Beck's Cognitive Therapy

Distinctive Features

Frank Wills

Routledge
Taylor & Francis Group

LONDON AND NEW YORK

First published 2009 by Routledge
27 Church Road, Hove, East Sussex BN3 2FA

Simultaneously published in the USA and Canada
by Routledge
270 Madison Avenue, New York, NY 10016

Routledge is an imprint of the Taylor & Francis Group,
an informa business

Typeset in Times by Garfield Morgan,
Swansea, West Glamorgan
Printed and bound in Great Britain by
TJ International Ltd, Padstow, Cornwall
Cover design by Sandra Heath

This publication has been produced with paper manufactured to
strict environmental standards and with pulp derived from
sustainable forests.

British Library Cataloguing in Publication Data
A catalogue record for this book is available from the British Library

Library of Congress Cataloging-in-Publication Data
Wills, Frank.
   Beck's cognitive therapy : distinctive features / Frank Wills. – 1st ed.
      p. cm.
   Includes bibliographical references and index.
   ISBN 978-0-415-43951-0 (hardback) – ISBN 978-0-415-43952-7
(pbk.) 1. Beck, Aaron T. 2. Cognitive therapy. I. Title.
   RC489.C63W54 2009
   616.89'1425–dc22

                                              2008036923

ISBN: 978-0-415-43951-0 (hbk)
ISBN: 978-0-415-43952-7 (pbk)

Contents

Acknowledgements

Much of this book was written as I completed my PhD at the University of Bristol – not a mode of writing that I would recommend to others! It did mean, however, that the book was sustained by the wit and wisdom of my supervisor, Dr William Turner, who I must thank not only for his support but also for his tolerance of my version of that old favourite – *PhD completion distress!*

Many others also contributed to the book's completion – my readers Dr Paul Hebblethwaite, Janet Grey, Stuart Matthews and Annie Wills; and my students, from whom I always learn so much. Thanks are also due to the editorial staff at Routledge and to Windy Dryden, for asking me to write it.

Introduction

> Take the anointing oil and pour it on Aaron's head, and
> anoint him. Then bring forward his children. . . . They will
> hold the priesthood for all time.
>
> (Exodus 29: 7–9)

In 1976, a 55-year-old David before Goliath, Aaron T. Beck
(1976, p. 333), asked, 'Can a fledgling psychotherapy challenge
the giants in the field – psychoanalysis and behavior therapy?'
Looking back now, 30 and more years later, the answer would
appear to be a resounding 'yes'. He has made an outstanding
contribution to the world of psychotherapy and counselling.
Along with Carl Rogers and Albert Ellis, he has been adjudged
to be one of the three most cited psychotherapy writers in the
literature. His daughter, Dr Judith Beck, whose work will also
be described in this book, has ably assisted him in recent years.
It is no small thing to launch a school of psychotherapy that
achieves international repute within one's lifetime. His
contribution comes not just from his own work but also from
a wide group of writers and researchers that he has nurtured
and encouraged to move on beyond him. Beck has always

enjoyed a close relationship with the UK, partly through programmes of mutual residencies between Philadelphia and Oxford. It may also be that the pragmatic yet independent-minded nature of cognitive therapy has chimed in well with certain traditions in UK psychotherapy, especially the distinctly pragmatic brand of behaviour therapy that had developed in Britain (Rachman, 1997a).

Beck has certainly proved an inspirational figure to a whole generation of thinkers and researchers. The pragmatic and empirical traditions within cognitive therapy have also seemed to resonate with the zeitgeist of the new millennium – one concerned with efficiency and, perhaps, iconoclasm.

Beck's life in brief

Born in 1921 to a Jewish family both sides of which had moved from Russia in the first decade of the twentieth century, Aaron Temkin Beck had serious childhood illnesses and a protective mother. Because he missed some early schooling through illness, he was for a time considered and even considered himself 'dumb', but, showing remarkable resilience and self-help, he moved forward to become a Yale-educated doctor. In retrospect, these experiences may have been excellent preparation for being a remarkably able and empathic doctor of the soul for anxiety and depression. At first, he wanted to specialise in neurology, but fate eventually and serendipitously steered his path toward psychiatry.

In 1953, psychiatrist Captain Beck, US Army, published one of his earliest papers – a study of five soldiers who had experienced psychotic depressive reactions after shooting and killing fellow soldiers in 'friendly fire' incidents in Korea. He was working in the Veterans Administration Hospital at Valley Forge (Pennsylvania), a name immortalised as the site of a famous camp of the American revolutionaries fighting the British in 1777. In many ways, Beck was a man with distinct Yankee characteristics despite the Russian-Jewish heritage.

Beck's paper (Beck & Valin, 1953) reflected the fact that he had been immersed in psychoanalytic treatment centres for some years – referring to the patients' possible 'unconscious hostility' to the buddies they had killed and to the 'defence mechanisms' used by them. There was also some flavour of the more cognitive concepts that were to emerge later – referring, for example, to the 'distortions' evident in the men's basic character make-up.

In 1954, he became an instructor at the University of Pennsylvania Medical School, a place he was to work in for over 40 years. He is reported to have been growing more ambivalent about psychoanalysis from this time, partly resulting from the disappointing results[1] of his own analysis. In 1959, this scepticism led him, now an associate professor, to study the dreams of depressed patients to test the validity of the psychoanalytic concept that depressed patients had a 'need to suffer'. The results of this research led to his breaking away from psychoanalysis, and what he found about depression led to the development of the cognitive therapy of depression. He regards the seeds of all his future work as having been laid down in the period 1960–64, when, in a series of typically elegant and thorough research papers, he identified the distinctive ideational content of depression (Beck, 1963, 1964) and then later anxiety (Beck et al., 1974b).

In 1967, he published the first of his ground-shifting books on depression (Beck, 1967). He wrote a particularly telling paper on the integration of cognitive therapy and behaviour therapy in 1970 (see Points 9, 10 and 14). A feature of Beck's work that was attractive to behaviour therapists was his emphasis on empirical outcome research (see Point 15). Behaviourists had pioneered the single-case study method based on measuring outcomes but mostly within fairly circumscribed areas, such as the phobias. During his depression research, Beck had devised what was to become the world-famous scale, the Beck Depression Inventory (Beck et al., 1961), setting the empirical tone of cognitive therapy. He later added the

Hopelessness Scale (Beck et al., 1974b), the Beck Anxiety Inventory (Beck et al., 1988) and, with David. A. Clark, the Clark–Beck Obsessive Compulsive Scale (Clark & Beck, 2002). These scales not only proved to be well-validated research scales but could also be used for identifying subtle issues in therapy (Padesky, 2004) and for relatively easy-to-implement ongoing evaluation by everyday practitioners.

Another strong area of contribution recognised the link between hopelessness and suicide. Depression was sustained by the 'cognitive triad': an interactive relationship between negative view of self, life and the future. Many clients could be quite depressed and yet retain hope that things might improve, but once hope receded, they could become highly vulnerable to suicide (Beck et al., 1975). Beck's team produced scales for suicidal intent (Beck et al., 1974b) and suicidal ideation (Beck et al., 1979a). Beck et al. (1979a) have a wonderfully clear and reassuring chapter on how therapists can best deal with suicidal clients. Beck's team went on to publish effective guidelines for identifying suicidal intent and intervening successfully (Brown et al., 2000; Weishaar & Beck, 1992).

In 1977, he was instrumental in setting up the journal *Cognitive Therapy and Research*, and its first edition contained a research study of the cognitive therapy of depression, which showed strong efficacy results (Rush & Watkins, 1977). As more results like this became available, cognitive therapy was hitting the headlines in the therapy world (Weishaar, 1993). This coincided with the publication of what is still probably the master text of cognitive therapy, *Cognitive Therapy of Depression* (Beck et al., 1979b).

Throughout his fifties, Beck began a veritable production line of influential books, chapters and articles. Padesky points out that he had 40 publications up to the age of 50 and 370 between 50 and 80. This increase was party due to his writing his 'big' books on depression in the 1960s and 1970s but also because he was being an attentive father. His down-to-earth and 'avuncular' nature has been noted by many (Goode, 2000)

– though it is also wise not to underestimate his sharp and tough mind (Weishaar, 1993). He withdrew his support for the grand-scale NIMH study of depression because he felt that the cognitive therapists in the trial were not properly trained and supervised. The results of the trial showed that cognitive therapy was effective, especially in follow-up, but was generally regarded as disappointing in the field (Hollon et al., 1996).

Beck began to work more with anxiety in the 1970s and 1980s. The cognitive therapy of anxiety also proved highly effective, especially with panic disorder, a field to which David M. Clark and his colleagues at Oxford made very significant contributions (Clark, 1996). Towards the end of the 1980s, he earned his first award with the Distinguished Scientific Award of the American Psychological Association in 1989. This was the first of many such awards. He became one of the most frequently cited authors in the psychotherapy literature and stood at second in 2005. During the late 1980s and 1990s, he expanded his work into new fields of application: couples work (Beck, 1988), personality disorders (Beck et al., 1990) and substance abuse (Beck et al., 1993).

In 1997, Beck suggested that cognitive therapy had secured its place in 'the arena of controversy' that is current psychotherapy. It had done this by establishing robust theories of psychopathology and effective treatments. He continued to work at the University of Pennsylvania and, showing characteristic energy, he also established his own Institute and Academy of Cognitive Therapy[2] and is still an active conference goer and inspirer of younger clinicians and researchers. As he has got older, he has been lucky to have his daughter, Judith, as an active collaborator and distinguished clinician and writer in her own right (Beck, 1995). They now work together as trainers and consultants at the Beck Institute centre in Philadelphia and throughout the world.

As Beck approached and passed his eightieth birthday and the new millennium unfolded, he continued to produce new and exciting material, written with his usual grace and clarity, on such problems as hate (Beck, 1999) and schizophrenia (Beck, 2004). This latter paper seemed to bring him almost full circle – schizophrenia had been the subject of one of his very first papers in 1952 – he will probably go round the whole circuit again now!

This book is structured into two parts; the first describes 15 of Beck's main contributions to the understanding of psychopathology, and the second, 15 of his main contributions to treatment. A critical perspective is maintained throughout, weighing strengths and weaknesses, and identifying gaps that still need further clarification or amendment. Beck has shown himself open to criticism and debate and indeed believes that the eventual evolution of his ideas will result in the successful incorporation of their best points into a standard model of psychotherapy, while the rest will be subject to gentle atrophy (Salkovskis, 1996b).

Describing Beck's contribution to the development of cognitive therapy is a demanding task for any author. He has done so much and moved so far, it has been hard to cover everything within Windy's editorial corset of Points and word length. Some of Beck's insights have become so integral to us that it is sometimes hard to detect the point at which he brought them in. Figure 1 presents a series of 'maps', ranging from the basic to the latest and most complex, that act as a guidepost to routes through his main written contributions.

So pack your sandwiches and put on your walking boots – let the journey commence.

Notes

1 Accounts of his analysis do differ somewhat.
2 Both the Academy and the Institute have excellent website sources of information about many aspects of cognitive therapy: www.academyofct.org and www.beckinstitute.org.

Period	Beginner's map	Intermediate's map Beginner's PLUS	Advanced map Beginner's and intermediate's PLUS
Early (1960–1978)	**Beck (1976):** First lengthy exposition of cognitive approach to psychopathology	**Beck (1963, 1964):** Foundational papers on the cognitive approach to depression	**Beck (1970a):** Early paper on imagery **Beck (1970b):** Influential paper on combining behaviour and cognitive therapy
Middle (1979–1994)	**Beck et al. (1979b):** Master text with first protocols on cognitive therapy of depression **Beck and Emery (1985):** Master text with first protocols on cognitive therapy of anxiety **Beck et al. (1990, 2004):** Outlines of cognitive therapy for personality disorders	**Beck (1988):** Interesting work on couples therapy and riposte to criticism implying he had overlooked interpersonal factors **Beck et al. (1993)** Outlines cognitive therapy of substance abuse	**Beck et al. (1975, 1979b):** Reviews of work on suicide **Beck (1991):** Article reviewing 30 years of cognitive therapy

Figure 1 Maps of Beck's main written contributions

Period	Beginner's map	Intermediate's map Beginner's PLUS	Advanced map Beginner's and intermediate's PLUS
Later (1995–2008)	**Salkovskis (1996b):** Chapter on interview with Beck on the development and future directions of cognitive therapy **Beck (2005a)** Article reviewing 40 years of cognitive therapy	**Beck (1995):** Shows some distinctive contributions of Judith Beck **Beck (1996):** Chapter on the development of the schema concept and evolutionary ideas **Alford and Beck (1997):** Argument for cognitive therapy as a meta-theory for psychotherapy	**Beck (1999):** Longer paper on evolutionary ideas **Beck et al. (2004):** Reviews work on cognitive therapy of schizophrenia **Beck (2005b):** Article on Buddhism and cognitive therapy

Figure 1 Continued

Part 1

THEORY

Prelude: Beck and his group

> Tim has been personally very good at spotting young, enthusiastic research people and then encouraging them enormously and helping them.
>
> (David M. Clark quoted in Weishaar, 1993, p. 41)

When Beck described his work at the University of Pennsylvania, he would invariably refer to the work of himself 'and our group'. At first this phrase seemed to refer to a group of talented therapists and researchers who helped him develop cognitive therapy: Jeff Young, Art Freeman, Mary Ann Layden, Steve Hollon and many others. Then, as the repute of his work grew, visitors came to Philadelphia to learn more and then proceeded to further the development in their own centres and countries: David Clark, Melanie Fennell, Adrian Wells and others. In both their own minds and in Beck's, people in the new centres often became 'in his group' and they then recruited and trained more therapists and researchers, many of whom saw themselves similarly. The 'group' therefore started to get quite large and would have defied the English football supporters' taunt to opposing fans, 'You're going home in a taxi.'[1] The largest Army formations are called 'Army Groups'; perhaps this is what Beck had in mind.

The happy consequences of this growing Beckian army have been that ideas developed by Beck have been expanded and filled out by others, resulting in a vibrant and innovative therapy community that in turn has often influenced other parts of the therapy field. As we review Beck's contributions, we will see the following pattern again and again: Beck develops a template idea, and it is taken further by both him and his wider group and often impacts on the wider world of therapy too. Collaboration, then, is not just a therapist quality but a way of being effective in the wider stage of the disciplines allied to psychological therapy (see Wills, 2008, Chapter 8).

Beckian epistemology ('way of knowing') is based on building interventions from solid conceptual foundations: we begin, then, by considering some of Beck's main contributions to the conceptual field of psychotherapy.

Note

1 There's so few of you that you could all fit into a taxi!

1

Cognitive therapy is organised around a formulation

The concept of formulation requires that therapists build the information collected about the client at assessment into a comprehensive model that explains the psychological factors involved in the development and maintenance of the client's problem. This 'formulation' is then used to guide and monitor psychological interventions. The notion of formulation has probably always been implicit in most approaches to therapy – evident, for example, in Freud's famous case studies – but it has evolved, especially in more recent years, by becoming more specific and explicit. A major step towards more explicit formulation came from ideas that developed in behaviour therapy in the 1960s and 1970s (Bruch & Bond, 1998), about the same time as the first prototypes of Beckian formulation were developing. Beck's formulations were based on 'cognitive specificity' (Point 2). Beck's cognitive model was firstly confined to depression (Beck et al., 1979b), but then, as interest grew following the success of that model, it was applied to other areas: to anxiety (Beck & Emery, 1985), personality disorders (Beck et al., 1990) and substance abuse (Beck et al., 1993). Explicitness grew from increasingly clearly written formulations presented in diagrammatic form. The diagram now most usually associated with cognitive therapy: the 'longitudinal formulation' (see Figure 2) seems to have been first drawn by Judith Beck (Beck, 1995). A template for full written formulations can be seen from the website of the Academy of Cognitive Therapy (www.academyofct.org).

One key feature of the way the Becks have developed formulation has been the way different types and levels of cognition have been elaborated and by the way relationships between them and other parts of client functioning have been postulated.

The most general and highest order level of cognition has been described as that of 'schema'[1] (Beck, 1964). A schema is regarded as a broad cluster of meanings that holds more specific core beliefs and assumptions. A core belief is an unconditional belief about the self, others or the world. An assumption is a conditional belief, often in the form of either an 'if–then' proposition or a rule of living (Beck, 1964). An example of this series of relationships might be as follows:

EARLY MALADJUSTED SCHEMA: *Mistrust* (Young et al., 2003).
NEGATIVE CORE BELIEF: *I cannot afford to trust anyone.*
UNHELPFUL ASSUMPTION: *If I trust someone, then I'll be let down.*

In longitudinal formulation, schemas, core beliefs and assumptions are seen as part of a vulnerability factor that predisposes clients to be triggered into negative symptoms and psychological problems. Life events trigger these latent negative patterns, and this often results in a self-maintaining 'vicious cycle' of negative thoughts, emotions and behaviour patterns, as shown in the lower part of Figure 2.

Jacqueline Persons (1989) uses a method of formulation that is slightly different from the Beckian 'longitudinal' format, but her work is nevertheless a useful bridge between the behavioural and cognitive traditions in formulation. Persons (1989) also presents some useful points on the many uses of formulation in CT/CBT: the formulation becomes the 'therapist's compass' and helps us to decide how to:

1 understand relationships among clients' problems
2 choose treatment modalities, interventions and starting points
3 make predictions of how clients may react to interventions and other events

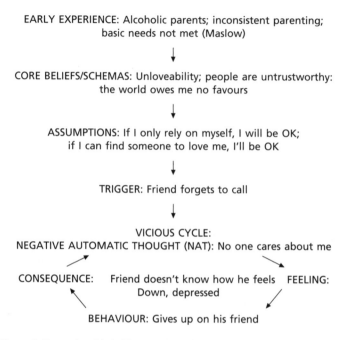

EARLY EXPERIENCE: Alcoholic parents; inconsistent parenting;
basic needs not met (Maslow)

↓

CORE BELIEFS/SCHEMAS: Unloveability; people are untrustworthy:
the world owes me no favours

↓

ASSUMPTIONS: If I only rely on myself, I will be OK;
if I can find someone to love me, I'll be OK

↓

TRIGGER: Friend forgets to call

↓

VICIOUS CYCLE:
NEGATIVE AUTOMATIC THOUGHT (NAT): No one cares about me

CONSEQUENCE: Friend doesn't know how he feels   FEELING:
Down, depressed

BEHAVIOUR: Gives up on his friend

Figure 2 Example of brief longitudinal formulation

4   manage problems in interpersonal relations between
     therapist and client in and outside therapy sessions
5   understand therapists' own reactions to particular clients
     and problems.

During the first few decades of its existence, use of the
longitudinal formulation model was hardly questioned. More
recently, however, more critical questions have been asked.
Bruch and Bond (1998), for example, have questioned whether
Persons' work has really presented the rigour of the behavioural
model she claims to build on. The idea that the rigour of
formulation can be tested has also been promoted by Willem
Kuyken (2006). Kuyken (2006, p. 12) wonders whether some of

the claims regarding the efficacy of formulations could be the 'emperor's new clothes'. He reviews research evidence on some of the 'haughty claims' (Kuyken, 2006, p. 31) made for the formulation concept and finds the data equivocal: studies have revealed only mixed interrater reliability for descriptive elements of formulation and much less for inferential elements. Kuyken (2006) suggests criteria that can be used to improve reliability to ensure 'good-enough' formulations, including a stress on humility and provisionality, as well as seeking harder evidence, such as might be gained from behavioural experiments.

Kuyken (2006) points out that the evidence base does mainly support the strong nomothetic (general) formulations for specific areas such as the depressive and anxiety disorders, but the same effort now needs to be made to look for evidence to support idiographic (individual) formulations.

To some extent, it could be argued that we should talk about 'cognitive therapies' rather than cognitive therapy. The 'cognitive specificity' hypothesis suggests that both the formulation and treatment of different disorders may be significantly different. Ironically, then, we might be said to be only doing cognitive therapy when working to individualised formulations. There is perhaps a danger that as CT/CBT spreads its wings wider and wider to more problem areas it could start to lose some of the parsimony of the original model. Wells (2006) therefore performs a valuable service by looking at the common elements in formulating the different anxiety disorders and pulling them into an over-arching process map for formulating any anxiety problem.

While Beck did not specifically invent the notion of formulation, there is no doubt that his work has given it a characteristically more specific format and that this format has provided a template for other therapy models to develop their own formats for formulation. There is increasingly convergence and increased specificity in the way different therapy models are using and presenting their formulations, and this is leading to the idea that the concept of formulation itself may emerge as a new 'common factor' in psychotherapy (Eells, 1997; Johnstone & Dallos, 2006).

Note

1 The usage of the plural form 'schemas' has been adopted by most CT/ CBT practitioners over the more technically correct Greek plural word, 'schemata'.

2

Different problem areas in cognitive therapy are marked out by specific cognitive themes

> A striking feature of the diverse application (viz. of cognitive therapy) has been the importance of cognitive specificity. Each disorder has its own specific conceptualisation[1] and relevant strategies that are embraced under the general principles of cognitive therapy.
>
> (Beck, 1991, p. 368)

The process of identifying the specific problem areas in cognitive therapy began one day during the late 1950s when Beck, then still practising psychoanalytic therapy, was listening to a client talk about her sexual experiences (Beck, 1976). She had previously done this without being upset but now suddenly expressed much distress and shed tears. An orthodox analytic stance would have suggested that the distress came from surfacing repressed feelings or memories, and yet she revealed nothing new. Curious, Beck began to ask her about her experiences and found that alongside her thoughts about her sexual experiences was a 'second stream' of thoughts, such as 'He will think badly of me' and 'I am boring him.' These types of thoughts Beck came to define as 'negative automatic thoughts' (NATs), and he began to find that they were omnipresent in the way that clients, when asked, described the inner process while experiencing psychological distress. The idea of a second stream of thoughts is similar to Albert Ellis's view, which sees clients as quite often having 'insane sentences' running parallel to their 'sane sentences' (Ellis, 1962). Sometimes these different thought streams may result from different processing systems that may operate somewhat independently. Epstein (1998), for example, refers to the 'rational' and the 'experiential' processing systems, and Teasdale (1996) refers to the 'propositional' and 'implicational' meaning systems. These different processing systems can help us understand conflicts between 'head and heart' – e.g., a client may say, 'I *know* I should give up, but I *feel* that I should go on.'

As he identified a widening array of NATs, Beck began to notice specific themes that varied according to the problem area being presented. Depressed clients, for example, reported NATs with the characteristic themes of loss (e.g., 'Nobody rates me anymore') and defeat ('I just wasn't up to the test'). Anxious clients, however, reported NATs that showed a preoccupation with impending danger or threat ('I will be blown away by this' and 'I won't be able to cope'). Hostile and angry clients reported thoughts showing a preoccupation with transgression and injustice. Transgressions might be sins of commission ('He treated me like dirt') or sins of omission ('She seemed to forget that I have needs as well').

The reader will note the frequent presence of interpersonal themes in these thoughts (Point 17) but should also note that they may be intrapersonal, especially in critiquing the self – e.g., 'I hate myself for being so weak' and 'I'm just a loser.' It is possible to note an implicit interpersonal theme in even these thoughts, however, as they often seem predicated on the existence of other people who are 'strong' and 'winners' and with whom the client may be comparing herself.

The 'cognitive specificity' template was extended by Beck and his group and then by others. Research findings have, by and large, verified these cognitive themes as significantly discernible between different client problem groups (Clark & Steer, 1996). The list of specific themes now includes, among others, the following:

Problem area:	Cognitive themes:	Researchers/authors:
Depression	Loss, defeat	Beck et al. (1979b)
Anxiety	Danger, threat	Beck & Emery (1985)
Panic	Physical, mental catastrophe	Clark (1996)
OCD	Inflated responsibility	Salkovskis (1991)
Substance abuse	Permissive beliefs	Beck et al. (1993)
Eating disorders	Self-criticism	Vitousek (1996)
Social anxiety	Fear of evaluation	Wells (1997)
PTSD	Impending threat	Ehlers & Clark (2000)

This simple table does not do justice to the full richness of the above descriptions of the 'cognitive architecture' of these problem areas, and readers are strongly encouraged to go back to the cited authors. The descriptions of the interior of the thinking processes of clients with these specific problems is an incredibly valuable treasure chest for practising clinicians, who should take the trouble to make themselves fully conversant with them.

The strong emphasis on cognitive content specificity is relatively unique to Beck's cognitive therapy. Rational emotive behaviour therapy (REBT) has focused more on general irrational beliefs, though some writers within the tradition have shown disorder-specific content relating to these beliefs (Dryden & Hill, 1992).

Clark and Steer (1996) argue that the cognitive content specificity hypothesis holds a crucial place in the theory and practice of cognitive therapy because it drives key elements of the therapist's interventions. While research has shown strong correlations between cognitive content and psychopathology, research efforts to test causal links have been less successful. Causality is of course a complex matter, and, as reported elsewhere in this book, cognitive therapy theory has increasingly adopted a 'stress-diathesis' model of causality. This model accepts that the aetiology of depression, for example, will involve many factors, cognitive and non-cognitive, and that not all these factors will operate in all depressed clients. Cognitive specificity themes, for example, tend to be more evident the stronger symptoms are.

The importance of the specificity hypothesis within approaches to aetiology is that it may act as a helpful guide for where therapists can look for intervention points. Wells (1997), for example, shows that clients with social anxiety have specific processing biases that reflect overly self-focused concern about what others may be thinking about them in social and performance situations. As social anxiety becomes apparent in the client, the therapist can therefore fruitfully ask about how the client is processing his perceptions of other people and their possible reactions to the client. The specificity model also suggests that helping socially anxious clients to review their processing biases will help them to master the accompanying anxiety symptoms. The working therapist effectively tests the validity of the specificity model each time he follows this sequence.

Note

1 The words 'conceptualisation' and 'formulation' carry the same meaning. I have recently decided to adopt 'formulation' because of the idea that it may emerge as the term for a new 'common factor', as described in the previous section.

3

Cognitive therapy varies according to the areas to which it is applied

> The aspiring cognitive therapist must be first a good psycho-therapist . . . The knowledgeable, warm, empathetic, accepting therapist . . . will need, in addition, to satisfy the following prerequisites:
>
> a A clear understanding of the cognitive model of depression . . .
> b A grasp of the conceptual framework of cognitive therapy . . . as well as its special application to the treatment of depression.
>
> (Beck et al., 1979b, p. 25)

Looking at the development of Beck's early and middle-stage work, we see a process of evolution which is quite different from many other models of therapy and different even from some types of cognitive behaviour therapy (CBT). Just the titles of his books tell us that he started by describing a way of working with depression (1979b), and then, having experienced some success with that work, tried the same principles with anxiety (Beck & Emery, 1985), relationship difficulties (1988), personality disorders (Beck, Freeman & Associates, 1990) and substance abuse (Beck et al., 1993). Notice, too, that he uses the phrase 'cognitive therapy'. The 'c' is lower case because it is an adjective; it has not yet hardened into a double-barrelled noun, 'Cognitive Therapy'. Beck also frequently uses the title style 'cognitive therapy of . . .,' not *The* Cognitive Therapy of . . .' Beck does not seem to have had a desire to construct a therapy school or model as such and that continues to be his position three decades later (Salkovskis, 1996b). Cognitive therapy therefore developed as a *style* of therapy which really only has a distinct meaning in relation to specific problems.

Some recent critics, thinking perhaps of the possible socio-political consequences of the plans to increase access to psychological therapy (Department of Health, 2008), have termed CBT 'imperialist'. In fact, cognitive therapy is potentially, the most self-limiting therapy model: it is literally only as much use as its applications and as its results. As a prime example of 'evidence-based practice', cognitive therapy may have to live with and die by that sword – namely, if sound outcome research starts to point to other, more effective forms of therapy, the cognitive therapist should have no hesitation in abandoning current methods and taking up these alternatives, no matter how close to or distant they may be from cognitive therapy methods. If it ever falters in the effectiveness stakes, it will quickly lose what might seem like its current imperial power. It is primarily a 'pragmatic' approach but is also less likely to follow some models' hazy application areas such as 'growth work' and 'life coaching'.

It seems likely that Beck initially had some hopes that his psychoanalytic colleagues might have been open to the cognitive style of therapy. One of the breaking points with psychoanalysis came from the fact that psychoanalytic thinking tended to espouse the same kinds of explanatory mechanisms for every problem and therefore developed very similar approaches to them all. As described in the previous section, what fascinated Beck, however, was how highly 'specific' and different were the styles of clients' thought processes when they were suffering from different disorders. The specificity was evident in diverse ways – for example, the thinking of a depressed client tended to be different from that of an anxious client. One type of client's anxiogenic thinking might, however, be different from that of another – a process of classification fusion and fission. In theory, the formulation and treatment of each client should be entirely idiographic and individual. In practice, however, there is always going to be overlap, and this is just as well for those of us who must learn and teach the model!

When I trained in working therapeutically with people with alcohol problems, a course tutor told us that once one had experienced working with 50 clients, one had 'met most of the variations of alcohol problems one was likely to meet'. I found this an encouraging idea and one that has been largely borne out by experience not only with alcohol problems but also in other major problem areas. Most therapists would be likely to encounter 50 clients at depth over a year or two, and it has been suggested that this is the period that is needed to master a specific treatment protocol (Wills, 2008). Such a view implies that while therapists should hold a healthy respect for individuality, there are patterns that can be discerned in terms of both understanding clients and then of changing things for them.

The test of the idea of semi-structured applications of cognitive therapy comes from discerning how specific formulations make clear differences in specific treatment approaches. For example, behavioural inactivity and withdrawal feature strongly in the formulation for cognitive therapy of depression. In the cognitive therapy of anxiety, however, behavioural interventions focus mainly on the problematic overactivation of safety behaviours. Interventions in the cognitive therapy of depression, therefore, feature behavioural activation, while the cognitive therapy of anxiety features the 'deactivation' of safety behaviours (Wills, 2008). Although the focus here is on behavioural problems and strategies, this behavioural focus will likely be reflected in the clients' cognitive organisations also: for example, through beliefs such as 'There is no point in trying' and 'If I go out alone, I will be in danger' in depression and anxiety, respectively. Even within anxiety disorders, there are specific differences in focus: on 'catastrophic misinterpretation' of body signals in panic (Clark, 1996) and on ruminative and meta-cognitive beliefs in generalised anxiety disorder (Wells, 1997). Although there are these clearly specific applications, it is well to remind ourselves that there will also frequently be the need for individualisation of formulation and treatment. The sheer frequency of co-morbidity also argues against the idea of specific formulation for all clients with the same problem.

Wells (1997) has argued for the need for more purely cognitive applications of cognitive therapy and conversely against the type of 'hybrid' models that can arise when techniques from other approaches are included in un-thought-out ways. More cognitively pure models are increasingly using new research on cognitive content and processes, as described elsewhere in this book:

> For cognitive therapy to evolve and for treatment effectiveness to increase, specific models of cognitive-behavioural factors associated with vulnerability and problem maintenance are required. . . . The aim . . . is the construction of a model that can be used for individual case conceptualisation for guiding the focus of interventions, and for generating testable model-based hypotheses.
>
> (Wells, 1997, p. 14)

4

Cognitive functioning is organised around the existence of deep schemas

We have already noted Beck's concept of psychopathology as having the nature of a 'stress-diathesis' ('stressor-vulnerability') concept. Such a model acknowledges that the aetiology of such complicated human problems as depression is likely to be multi-causal. Multi-causal factors are likely to be many but may be conveniently grouped into two main categories: firstly, stressors – current life events – that act as triggers for the second set of factors – connected with underlying vulner-abilities. Having been criticised for overstressing the role of current cognitions (Weishaar, 1993), Beck clarified that cognitive factors were only one set of factors in his 1991 paper on depression. According to this paper, underlying factors were likely to include life and socio-economic factors, physiology, health and genetics, as well as the cognitive factors that he had mapped so carefully in his key publications on depression (Beck, 1967; Beck et al., 1979b). He nonetheless argued, and has continued to argue since, that cognitive factors play a lynchpin role in determining the way the depressive reaction unfolds. In the next Point – 5 – we will look at another set of underlying factors proposed by Beck: those connected with evolutionary theory. In Points 6–9, we will examine various layers or levels of cognition (core beliefs, assumptions and automatic thoughts) and the way they are involved – alongside the matter of consideration in this section – schemas – in the activation and maintenance of the symptoms of psychopathology.

A schema is hypothesised to be a general cognitive structure in which experiences, memories, thoughts, attitudes and beliefs connected with a cluster of generalised meaning gather (Beck, 1964). Schemas are intrinsically neither good nor bad, though, because the term is often used by cognitive therapists as a short-hand term for 'early maladaptive schema' (Young et al., 2003), it is often associated in therapeutic discourse with psychological problems. A schema might, however, contain a generally positive meaning cluster, such as 'I am an OK person', 'People who know me, generally like me', and 'Even people who don't know me will generally give me a chance'. We might sum this up as a 'lovability schema'. As might be expected, however, such a schema is much less commonly found in therapy clients than its opposite, 'un-lovability schema' (Young et al., 2003). The content of schemas is less conscious and specific than that for automatic thoughts and is perhaps best thought of as consisting of 'schematic elements'. These may well be related to early, even very early experience and because of this may have not been encoded in language. Because of the psychoanalytic associations of the word 'unconscious' and perhaps also because of the potential for the reification (taking an abstract concept and making it sound more concrete and actual than it really is) of the term in psychoanalytic discourse, cognitive therapists have generally preferred the term 'non-conscious'. Schematic triggering may be promoted by associations with early traumatic experience by sensation, touch, sound and smell, as well as by language, in much the same way that a traumatised soldier can be triggered into shock by the sound of car exhaust backfiring and sounding like a rifle shot. The person carrying the vulnerability is usually not continually triggered into experiencing symptoms, but the schema may act as 'an accident looking for somewhere to happen' when the wrong sets of events and sensations come together.

A restimulation effect is seen as a 'bottom-up' effect that comes surging up from the underlying factor and suffuses itself into the current reaction, overloading it with unmanageable negative feelings and symptoms (Wills, 2008). It is possible to use a metaphor from electricity to understand restimulation: a client may be able to withstand a 50-volt shock of negative feeling. A bad current event that generates 50 volts of shock may therefore be manageable. If the current experience stimulates a previous bad experience, then a further number of volts may come surging through into the client's mind and may therefore lead to overload and unmanageable distress. This understanding of restimulated distress in schematic functioning has face validity for therapists and is usually quite plausible to clients but has proved the very Devil's own job for the researchers to demonstrate. Various researchers have tried to demonstrate the kind of biases in cognitive processing that schema theory would predict. The results have been quite mixed and difficult to interpret (Wells, 2000). Wells (2000) points out that this research has proceeded mainly by self-report data, known to limit the validity of data, especially perhaps with a phenomenon where some non-conscious processing is suspected. Another major problem is the circularity of the way in which latent schemas are suggested to operate: sometimes biases are claimed as a by-product of schemas and sometimes as an influence on them. This latter dilemma is reinforced by the fact that schema effects are most demonstrable during the acute phase of a disorder and least demonstrable during remission.

More recent schema research has focused on a network concept. Teasdale (1996), for example, describes an 'interacting cognitive subsystems' network in which all kinds of current and previous experiences may interact with different reaction and symptom systems to produce schematic distress reactions. The results of this kind of set of subsystems are necessarily more complex than the original simpler schema concept but may be uncovered by careful empirical investigation over time. Beck (1996) revised his thoughts on schemas to suggest that their operation might resemble a network of different types of reaction related to evolutionary 'modes'. Both Beck (1996) and Teasdale (1996) have acknowledged the similarity of their respected revised schema theories.

5

It is helpful to understand the evolutionary underpinnings of psychological problems

> The evolutionary model views depression as an atavistic mechanism or program that may have been adaptational in a prehistoric environment but is not adaptive in our current milieu.
>
> (Beck, 2002, pp. 29–30)

Such an approach has been partly stimulated by the problems surrounding the nature of the schema concept. Some critics have pointed to the weakness that there is a lack of a convincing underlying theory about why cognitive therapy works. On one level, many cognitive therapists might not have a great need for a theory that explains everything and might be happy to be considered as pragmatists.[1] Beck (1996) has, however, speculated about the links between cognitive processing and evolutionary mechanisms and has been joined by other writers such as Paul Gilbert (2006).

The schema concept has a similarity to the evolutionary concept of Bowlby, who describes attachment as 'a working model' in the mind that has pronounced survival value for helpless neonates. Beck (1987) recognised the need to include the concept of attachment in the theory of depression, showing that sociotrophic individuals with greater needs for relationships tend to react differently to loss of relationship than more autonomous individuals. The Italian school of cognitive therapy has been particularly prominent in elaborating the implications of attachment for CBT (Liotti, 1991, 2007).

Beck has also written intriguingly about the survival value of certain psychological 'problems'. Anxiety, for example, with its attendant 'safety behaviours', such as extra vigilance against danger, worrying about future threats, and checking that necessary precautions have been taken, may, at least up to a point, enhance survival (Beck & Emery, 1985). Anxiety sufferers develop heightened awareness of danger to keep themselves safe but at the cost of risking many false positives (believing danger exists when it does not). We could, for example, have a burglar alarm that reacts to the slightest movement in or near the house – thus potential burglars would always be spotted but at the cost of keeping us awake half the night.

Beck and Emery (1985) see anxiety as being functional in detecting and reacting to threat. Most people can switch to appropriate activation and deactivation of normal anxiety most of the time. Anxiety sufferers, however, seem to have developed a 'cognitive set' that over-stresses defensiveness and vigilance. The set may link with an 'anxious mode' that prolongs anxious functioning. The problem is not so much that anxiety is invoked[2] but that it is not switched off when a proper appraisal of the actual danger has been made. Switching the anxiety mechanism on gives all the physical and mental backup that may be needed for 'fight or flight', but these heightened feelings become counter-productive once the danger has either ended or been appraised as not immediately present. The task for anxiety sufferers therefore becomes to learn to appropriately switch off anxiety and worry. They are frequently suppressing worry immediately rather than switching it off in a well-considered way. Suppression has the paradoxical effect of strengthening anxiety, perhaps because it does not allow time for the threat to be realistically appraised. An approach that recommends learning to 'switch off anxiety' makes sense to many clients and, in my view, is quite normalising and non-stigmatising.

Beck (1987) has also applied evolutionary thinking to depression, emphasising the advantage of a 'closing down' response after some types of loss and defeat. If one is truly defeated, then submission may be needed to prevent further attack. If one's attachment figure truly is lost, then it is often better to go into a transitional period of withdrawal rather than giving up completely or committing to another attachment too quickly. This has sometimes been called a 'hibernation effect': conserving emotional energy and behavioural activity in order to survive a hard winter. The problem comes, however, when the sufferer is unable to re-emerge into the sunlight of spring – rather like the switch problem in anxiety, the withdrawal switch is stuck in the on position.

Beck, Freeman & Associates (1990) also applied evolutionary analysis to personality disorders and describes 'ethological strategies' that may appear problematic but might at some times have survival value. Dependence, for example, can be functional for a time when one is genuinely incapacitated, but as a more permanent behaviour trait it may turn toward dependent personality disorder, which is defined by inability 'to make everyday decisions without an excessive amount of advice or reassurance from others' (American Psychiatric Association, APA, 2000 (DSM-IV-TR), p. 284). Even the rigidity of obsessive compulsive disorder (OCD) personality disorder may have positive adaptational value in some situations, such as where there might be the need to keep checking for the possible development of a dangerous situation (Beck et al., 1990).

In summary and in critical review of Beck's contribution to this debate, one might say that he has provided intriguing insights into the role that evolutionary theory could play in cognitive therapy but that neither he or even any of his 'wider group' have yet laid down a thorough-going theoretical framework. The fullest attempts have been those of Paul Gilbert (1989, 1998, 2007). One surprising aspect of this has been the lack of dialogue between evolutionary approaches to cognitive therapy and the wider movements of 'evolutionary psychology' and 'evolutionary psychiatry'. In one way, these are unfair criticisms – we can hardly expect Beck to account for everything and dialogue with everyone involved in everything's description! The situation also needs to be viewed in the light of the perhaps lamentable narrowing of academic and intellectual life where relatively small groups of people pursue increasingly specialised domains of knowledge in specialised languages designed to keep others out. Beck's contribution to psychotherapy has been incredibly broad and inclusive enough for one lifetime perhaps.

Notes

1 'I think I am ultimately a pragmatist and if it doesn't work, I don't do it' (Beck, quoted in Goode, 2000).
2 I sometimes say to clients that anxiety shows the equipment is still working.

6

Beck has described a variety of levels and types of cognition

Much of the initial impact of cognitive therapy came from Beck's concept of negative automatic thoughts (NATs). As often happens, simplified versions of cognitive therapy circulated in the therapy world, and these may have been overfocused on the importance of NATs, which were after all, phenomena that most people could get hold of and use without vast amounts of training. In addition, as Alford and Beck (1997, p. 67) put it:

Cognitive therapy originated in a context of pragmatic exigencies associated with clinical practice.

In such a context, some theoretical constructs lay implicit in the model and only became more fully explicated in later days as Beck became less embroiled in everyday practice. This was particularly true of the concept of 'cognitive organisation', frequently mentioned yet not much described in Beck's early works. Alford and Beck (1997) supply a fuller explanation of the nature of cognitive organisation. They acknowledge that Beck was influenced by Freud's concept of primary and secondary processes but describe the levels of functioning in cognitive therapy theory as following:

Cognitive theory stipulates 3 cognitive systems (or levels); 1) the preconscious, unintentional, automatic level, 2) the conscious level, and 3) the meta-cognitive level.

(Alford & Beck, 1997, p. 65)

Here, however, we will focus on the content aspect of these levels and will consider the aspects relating to cognitive processes in Points 11–13.

Beck (1963, 1976) considers the nature of NATs. They are negative because they tend to result in negative emotions and actions from the person who has them. They are automatic because they typically seem to come very quickly into the mind, without conscious effort. The individual may not even be immediately aware of having them. The speed at which they pass through the mind means that they often evade immediate critical review, and this may make them seem more plausible than they deserve.

As Beck was developing this concept during his days of psychoanalytic practice, he was able to check the NATs of clients with other material such as verbatim accounts of their 'free associations' during analysis. He found that the themes evident in NATs hardly ever occurred in free association. This absence led to an important rule of practice – you have to ask about NATs and about images containing NATs (Beck, 1976). The need to ask also perhaps justified one of his favourite maxims: 'There's more to the surface than meets the eye' (Goode, 2000). NATs are also specific, discrete and often delivered in shorthand style – e.g., 'That was rubbish'. He noted that the themes in the thoughts were idiosyncratic but also tended to show clusters of meaning that could be linked to other clients with the same disorder – taking him towards the specificity concept. Although they showed pronounced 'distortions', they were highly believable to patients, especially when they were experiencing negative emotional arousal.

Even when a NAT surfaces, however, there is still the issue of what that thought *means* – and this may not always be directly stated in the thought. For example, when a distressing event occurs, many people will describe their NAT as 'Why me?' This NAT may well be disguising another thought such as 'I am a loser', or, 'my life is doomed'. The therapist can get at these underlying meanings by asking clients how they would answer the question that they are asking themselves. There is an obvious danger here, however, in that the therapist can 'fish' for content too avidly and may lead a compliant client to give what the therapist seems to want. This is a delicate line along which therapists must tread. The ideal solution is to work mostly with verbatim client content, but the salient material can sometimes be somewhat hidden or difficult to express and the client may need help to bring it out.

Beck (1976) devotes considerable effort to clarify that it is really the *meaning* in cognition that carries the action in which therapists are likely to be interested. Focus on meaning parallels that of existential therapists (Van Deurzen-Smith, 2002). Once meaning is considered, then the content of cognition moves closer to being connected to beliefs, a different order of cognition than automatic thoughts. In his review of the development of cognitive therapy theory in its first 30 years, Beck (1991, p. 372) describes this relationship between thoughts and beliefs:

> The internal representation of the meanings evoked by the symbols constitutes a network of beliefs, assumptions, formulas, and rules . . . the relevant beliefs interact with the symbolic situation to produce the 'automatic thoughts'.

Beliefs are therefore a higher order level of cognition than thoughts but shape the content of thoughts. Initially, there was no distinction between different types of beliefs, but, over time, Beck started to distinguish between unconditional core beliefs and conditional assumptions. Judith Beck (1995) crystallised a way of drawing up longitudinal formulations of these different layers of cognition triggering into each other (see Figure 3).

Core beliefs are sometimes compared to the roots of a tree: a cognitive tree, as it were. They give rise to a trunk (intermediate beliefs), branches (assumptions) and leaves (automatic thoughts). It is important for therapists to be clear about the relationship between these different levels of cognition

SCHEMA: provide the general 'feel' of the situation as perceived by mind, senses and 'gut feeling'.

CORE BELIEFS: Supply the belief content of the schemas, often in basic 'black and white' terms (I am good or I am bad) and orientate the person towards self, others and the universe/future.

UNHELPFUL ASSUMPTIONS: Because the unconditional nature of core beliefs makes them uncompromising to hold (if one is bad, what is the point of trying anything?), assumptions may try to compensate for them and to make it worthwhile at least trying: e.g., ' I may be bad but if I can get people to like me somehow, then I can be OK' (conditional beliefs). These new rules, however, carry the hazard of dealing with the actuality of people not liking one and therefore of seeing oneself as, by definition, 'not OK'.

NEGATIVE THOUGHTS: If schemas and beliefs are the chiefs of the cognitions tribe, NATs are the 'injuns' – ready to perform their negative duties at all times of day and night and in all weathers.

Figure 3 The nature and relationship of different levels of negative cognitions

organisation. Changing different types of cognitions does tend to require different types of cognitive restructuring. As is shown in Part 2, automatic thoughts are generally tackled via thought records, whereas core beliefs are tackled via historical tests, the continuum technique and positive data logs (Padesky & Greenberger, 1995; Wills, 2008). These different methods also take account of the different time scales over which thoughts and beliefs have developed and during which they can reasonably be modified. Clients can see quite rapid changes in thinking and mood by using thought records. Frequent use of thought records additionally produces change on a more continuous basis.

Progress on modifying core beliefs and schemas is typically much slower. Negative beliefs and assumptions may have built up over many years so that they can just seem to be the way the world and life actually are. Here the 'drip, drip' effect is the main style of cognitive change: for example, when clients are asked to keep a positive data log, they will be collecting positive information about themselves and their lives, something that has been consistently disregarded in previous functioning. The client can find this a very difficult thing to do and typically requires a good deal of encouragement to stay with the task. Mary Ann Layden (1998) has made the analogy that asking a client who has habitually thought of herself as a 'bad person' to consider that she might have good aspects is like asking a person whether she would like to go to live on the moon.

Negative core beliefs become more central to cognitive therapy with personality-based problems (Beck, Freeman & Associates, 1990; Layden et al., 1993) and in schema-focused work (Young et al., 2003). These authors have given useful tools to other therapists by delineating the architecture of core beliefs and schemas. Beck, Freeman and Associates (1990) give especially clear lists of typical core beliefs associated with different problem areas, and these beliefs seem to map quite well onto the beliefs described in the schema questionnaires developed by Young and his colleagues.

7

Cognitive distortions play a key role in emotional problems but are not necessarily 'irrational'

A crucial element in the development of the understanding of how negative thoughts operate in depression, and then in other psychological problems was the identification of distorting tendencies likely to promote 'cognitive errors' on the part of the sufferer. Beck (1976) distinguishes these distortions from 'delusions' of more psychotic illnesses but also sees the two phenomena as being on the same continuum with the degree of distortion and error increasing the more severe the symptoms become. Beck (1963, 1976) identified various types of distortion – for example, 'personalisation' and 'polarised thinking', and their number was gradually expanded in succeeding publications (Beck et al., 1979b; Beck & Emery, 1985) to become a list of cognitive distortions that became standard in cognitive therapy texts thereafter, including:

- *Overgeneralisation*: the client typically describes a higher ratio of his experiences as negative than is really the case.
- *Arbitrary inference*: the client typically latches on to one particular negative view of her situation.
- *Selective abstraction*: the client typically picks out one negative slice of information and ignores other more positive factors.
- *Tunnel vision*: the client typically focuses on a very narrow range of factors that are likely to confirm his negative overall view.
- *Black and white thinking*: the client typically pushes neutral, 'grey' information into the category of the negative.

- *Should statements*: the client typically has self rules which demand high and perfectionist standards from herself.
- *Magical thinking*: the client typically imagines that his 'badness' is transparent to all.
- *Catastrophising*: the client typically over-exaggerates the potential dangers existing in everyday situations.
- *Labelling*: the client typically accentuates negative aspects of a situation or a person by attaching a stereotypical negative label to them.

I have found in both my practice and training that there seems to be a fair degree of overlap in these categories, and this is sometimes confusing to trainees if they try to identify them in a way that overemphasises their discrete quality (Wills, 2008). It can be useful to distinguish them because some clients do seem to have 'favourite' distortions. It seems, however, more useful to try to use simplified versions of distortions where main themes are identified (Emery, 1999; Wills, 2008).

Beck has advanced the understanding of negative cognition by disassembling it into parts, whereas his writings have also stressed that these parts, such as cognitive distortions, are firmly part of a holistic cognitive organisation. Alford and Beck (1997), for example, have described a fixated quality of negative cognitions, and this quality ensures that clients get 'locked on to' this negative material. It can be seen that most of the distortions in the above list result in (or is it from?) negative attention bias: a factor that only adds to the compulsive plausibility of negative thinking described in the above sections on the nature of NATs.

One point on which Beck and Ellis appear to disagree is on whether negative automatic thoughts are 'irrational' (Ellis) or 'dysfunctional' (Beck). While on one level, this is a rather semantic difference, it can be to some extent seen as an inappropriate comparison of levels of cognition: Ellis's concept is about 'beliefs', whereas Beck's automatic thought concept may represent 'inferences' based on those beliefs. Beck (1991), however, stresses that it is actually 'belief change' that leads to therapeutic change, implying that a process of modifying thoughts begins to alter the higher-order beliefs of which they are an outcrop. Beck has stressed the idiosyncratic nature of client beliefs and has advocated a methodology of empirically testing how well these work for clients in pursuing their life goals and avoiding psychological problems. This is essentially a more pragmatic style than that of the rational emotion behaviour therapy (REBT) advocated by Ellis, which stresses the need to confront and dispute 'irrational' client beliefs that tend to be conceived in terms of predefined beliefs from the 'dirty dozen' beliefs held to underlie many client problems. These beliefs include the following:

> I must be loved and approved of by everyone.
>
> (Edelman, 2006)

It might, however, be noted that Ellis (1979) has disputed the fact that REBT gives preferential weight to confronting such beliefs. It may also be that CT and REBT strategies are not necessarily incompatible – there is little empirical evidence of their relative effectiveness. Their different strategies may represent temperamental differences between their leading authors. It sometimes falls to pioneers of therapeutic approaches to advocate more starkly distinct versions of their ideas in order to clarify their difference from other approaches. Exponents of REBT in particular have sometimes appeared to relish their reputation as the 'roughnecks' of the therapy world (Dryden, 1998). Differences between the ways in which the therapies are conducted on the ground are, from my observations, not nearly so pronounced. In clarifying his difference with Ellis, however, Beck does suggest that it may not be useful to think of a client's beliefs as 'irrational'. The labelling of client phenomena can impact on the therapeutic enterprise, and I would argue that for many clients, the word 'unhelpful' is a more effective term than either 'irrational' or 'dysfunctional'. On the other hand, REBT also prides itself on its robustness and vigour, and sometimes it is necessary to confront unhelpful beliefs quite forcefully. Padesky and Beck (2003) have suggested that this difference marks the central philosophical concern of REBT, but Ellis himself has rejected this point.

8

Images also contain key elements of cognitions distortions

> The more he believes in the reality of the danger, the greater is his anxiety. At times, the fantasy may be so powerful that the patient may lose cognizance of the fact that he is not actually in the phobic situation. . . . Many patients report that their fantasy experiences are almost identical with the actual situational experiences. The patient may *live through* the frightening event in much the same way that a patient with a combat neurosis relives (abreacts) a combat experience under amytal.
>
> (Beck, 1976, p. 327)

The reference to imagery in the above quotation is intriguing and follows on from the thinking of an early paper on the use of imagery in cognitive therapy (Beck, 1970a). This was one of two key and original contributions made by Beck in 1970. The other was a paper on the relationship between cognitive therapy and behaviour therapy (Beck, 1970b). Although many people might associate the use of imagery with humanistic therapy, in fact the usage discussed by Beck (1970a) comes from a tradition of imagery use in behaviour therapy that follows the theoretical contributions of Lang (1977) – especially in relation to the role of imagery in anxiety and treatment methods based on desensitisation. Beck and Emery (1985) discuss how preoccupied anxious clients may become with their negative imagery – running what one might call a 'catastrophic movie' with much detail each time they approach or think about an anxiety-provoking situation. This is an example of what Alford and Beck (1997, p. 20) referred to as 'transfixed attention'.

Beck considered that his work on imagery in the 1970 paper was at first rather ignored by therapists (Weishaar, 1993), and it was a later generation of therapists that began to develop imagery more. One key exponent of the use of imagery has been Judith Beck, who devotes a comprehensive chapter to it (Beck, 1995). Judith Beck (1995, p. 229) notes that images occur spontaneously in therapy but can also be specifically induced for therapeutic purposes. It is not enough merely to identify them:

Failure to identify and *respond* to upsetting images may result in continued distress for the patient (italics added).

The experience of imagery may be very fleeting, so that it is important for the therapist to keep asking about them and to stay with them once they have been elicited. Alford and Beck (1997, p. 70) use Epstein's 'cognitive-experiential self' model (see also Point 2) to argue that guided imagery has two functions:

1) It activates meta-cognitive (rational) processing, and, 2) It is employed clinically to communicate with the experiential (automatic) system.

Staying with the image can give time for the slower rational processing system to 'fine-tune' what is happening in the more rapidly functioning experiential system. Beck (1970a) noted that interruption of negative imagery as part of a deliberate imagery exercise often results in the emergence of a positive image when the exercise is recommenced. Beck (1970a) describes how the client can be encouraged to disengage from such images by imagining a bell or whistle with the signal stop and how this disengagement often leads to a drop in anxiety. Beck and Emery (1985) also describe how encouraging the client to reactivate the closed-down image then elicits more positive detail and meaning.

Like NATs, the content of imagery can be highly specific. Wells (1997) gives interesting examples of the variation of images that occur to clients with social anxiety. Such clients tend to have detailed images of how they think people in social situations react to them. Sometimes these images are seen from an observer perspective – the client sees himself looking embarrassed. This contrasts with images that are seen from the perspective of the self – i.e., in this instance, the client sees the other people reacting as if he were looking embarrassed. The presence of the observer perspective in the imagery of a socially anxious client indicates the desirability of using attentional strategies to help the client to focus attention away from such self-focused processing, rather than the process of 'staying with the image'.

Judith Beck (1995, p. 233) refers to the process of staying with, interrupting and recommencing imagery as 'following images to completion'. She also describes ways of getting clients to imagine coping successfully with situations that they find difficult. Other therapists, such as Layden et al. (1993) and Hackmann and Holmes (2004), have followed the lead of Edwards (1990) in using active imagery rescripting of painful childhood and other traumatic experiences.

It can be helpful for the client to be encouraged to 'unpack' the detail of the image (Hackmann & Holmes, 2004). As described in the quotation at the start of this section, the cognitive content of the image adds to the vivid impact of the negative meaning contained within. One of my depressed clients vividly imagined being rejected at a job interview, and this led her to give up on any intention to apply. The detail contained in the imaginary sequence was surprisingly elaborate – the client even imagined her interviewers pulling faces as they looked at her application. It is hardly surprising that such vivid imagery captures the client's attention. There is evidence that when people imagine certain events strongly enough their bodies may react in a way that is very similar to the way they would in an actual situation. To some degree, when the client in the above example had the image of her 'interview', she suffered in a way similar to that in which she would have had she actually been rejected for the job. The end result was the worst of all worlds – she was 'rejected' without ever having had a chance to succeed.

Layden et al. (1993) describe work with clients with borderline personality disorder. These clients often have very intense emotional reactions, which can both help and hinder imagery work. Layden et al. (1993) recommend combining imagery work with techniques to modulate intense affect, because the emotional reaction can be so strong as to throw therapeutic work off track. Layden et al. (1993) describe a wealth of ways of working creatively with traumatic imagery, including importing a helpful 'safe adult' friend into the image and running the scene again and allowing the 'adult self' or 'empowered child' to come to the aid of the 'child self' in the childhood trauma. Imagery associated with early painful memories can be influenced by what Layden et al. (1993, p. 90) call 'the cloud' – a melange of painful and visceral memory and experience – the exploration of which is potentially difficult but rewarding work. Speaking of the abused person's characteristic tendency to blame himself, Layden et al. (1993, p. 86) comment:

> Metaphorically speaking, the 'child' remains convinced that the abuse is his fault. . . . Once the adult patient is capable of understanding rationally that he is not to blame for the abuse . . . the process of trying to convince the 'child' of his innocence with imagery exercises may begin.

We can see, once again, how a concept elicited by Beck has been taken up and developed both by him and by other therapists. The use of imagery in cognitive therapy has been developed and deepened by this process, and Beck himself has appeared happy to endorse the work of those who have followed by using it in his own work with clients with similar problems (Beck, Freeman & Associates, 1990).

9

Cognition, emotion and behaviour interact with mutual and reciprocal influence on each other

Beck saw the nature of emotion and how it would be handled in cognitive therapy as having two key elements (Weishaar, 1993, p. 57):

Emotion is a source of information about how the self is being affected by the environment and is affecting the environment.

And

Emotion is also part of the action tendency that helps to motivate adaptive behaviour.

Beck has frequently argued that emotion is extremely important in cognitive therapy because it is 'where the action is'. For example, the therapist can know that she is targeting the most salient and meaningful cognitions when the client shows a distinct emotional reaction to the 'hot thought'. Beck (1976) has linked this kind of salient reaction to what is most centrally important to the client. When a trigger hits a very meaningful area to individuals, it is more likely to register an impact on their personal domain.

Beck, however, did not follow Ellis in deciding to include the word 'emotion' within the rubric title of the therapy and has sometimes said that the word emotion does not need to be stated there because it was a symptom target – i.e., the cognitive therapy of *depression*.

Emotion is crucial in CBT. The emotions associated with problems such as anxiety and depression are conceptualised as continuous rather than categorical variables. Emotions must also have a cognitive appraisal element – linked to the 'personal domain' concept and cognitive specificity.

Some of the many ways that therapists of other schools have misunderstood CBT have been connected with the role of emotions in cognitive therapy. Firstly, it has been suggested that a focus on cognition implies a lack of interest in emotion in therapy. Christine Padesky (1994) tells an excellent story about Beck's exposition of the relationship between thoughts and feelings and the story also shows the impish dimension of Beck's character.[1] She and Beck were giving a workshop to one group in the morning and repeating the same workshop to psychoanalysts in the evening.

> We did one workshop in the morning and he said, 'Affect is the royal road to cognition.' He was talking about how you can't do cognitive therapy without affect being present. . . . Later in the evening . . . he said, 'Cognition is the royal road to affect.' I just looked at him and smiled as he turned the message round to fit his audience, but, in fact, both were true. Affect and cognition are wedded to each other, so that you can use affect to help you figure out and guide you to cognition, you can also use cognition to help you figure out and guide you to affect.
>
> (Padesky, 1994)

The key idea here is that 'emotion is where the action is' and that cognition is mostly useful because it explains the appraising and evaluative dimensions that are key to understanding problematic feelings and behaviours.

Recent writers on CBT such as Leahy (2003) have suggested that some elements from emotion-focused therapy (Greenberg, 2002, 2007) can be helpfully used in cognitive therapy. Wills (2008) has given examples of how focusing on emotions by some of the methods suggested by Gendlin (1981) and similar authors can be part of a wider approach to 'cognitive-emotional processing'.

Beck took some aspects of Ellis' ABC concept into his model and was particularly careful to include the behavioural consequences of unhelpful cognitions and beliefs. Reflecting on this period, Beck (1976, pp. 335–336) commented:

> Behaviour therapy appeared at a propitious time for me. The behavior therapists' emphasis on eliciting precise data from the patient, the systematic formulation of a treatment plan, the careful monitoring of feedback from the patient, and the refined methods of quantifying behavioural change were all useful tools in developing cognitive therapy. . . . [however] Insofar as the techniques of behavior therapy are employed [it is] with the perspective of a cognitive model.

Beck drew on research that showed that much of the success of Wolpe's (1958) systematic desensitization procedure was due to the changes in the client's attitudes (Brown, 1967). This drew an entertainingly robust and anti-cognitivist response from Wolpe himself (Wolpe, 1978) and characteristically even-tempered and clever respective rejoinders from both Beck (1979) and Ellis (1979).[2]

Beck's (1970b) key paper on behaviour therapy had made explicit attempts to link up some aspects of cognitive therapy with it. A particular feature of this was the understanding that behaviour change and cognitive change could reinforce each other. If you believe that if other people get to know certain things about you they will not like you, then you are not likely to tell people those things. If you do tell them, however, and people do still like you, then that belief is disconfirmed. A special application of understanding the relationship between behaviour and cognition came from Beck's work with the anxiety disorders, where he was able to identify key behaviours that reinforce anxiety: specifically avoidance, reassurance seeking, hyper-vigilance and what was later termed 'safety behaviour'

(Salkovskis, 1996a). The role of behavioural responses in both anxiety and depression provides the theoretical underpinning of the 'behavioural experiment' discussed in Point 29. Whereas behavioural interventions in the treatment of anxiety work mostly on trying to deactivate certain behaviours that reinforce the anxiety reaction syndrome, the behavioural interventions in depression work on activating behaviour. Beck was also able to build on the work of Lewinsohn to promote more active and pleasure-seeking behaviours (Lewinsohn & Graf, 1973) to get depressed clients 'up and running again'. Beck's integration of behavioural and cognitive interventions has played a crucial role in the integration of CBT (Rachman, 1997a).

Notes

1 Humour is evident in his tapes and books also. I agree that judicious use of humour can have powerful positive effects in therapy (Beck et al., 1979b, pp. 71–72).
2 These three articles are particularly recommended to those who relish a good academic spat.

10

Safety behaviours, including avoidance, reassurance seeking and hyper-vigilance, play a crucial role in maintaining anxiety

Beck carried his concept of 'dysfunctional thinking' into his work on the anxiety disorders (Beck & Emery, 1985). While depressogenic thinking seemed so central in depression, anxiogenic thinking was clearly accompanied by other very significant phenomena, including sharp and strong physiological reactions and behavioural responses based on 'fight or flight'. It is natural to feel uncomfortable at the prospect of unpleasant experiences, and it seems natural to choose one of the three main 'safety behaviours' – avoidance, escape or active (positive or negative) coping. The positive coping behaviour is to advance towards the anxiety-provoking stimulus – the only known way of overcoming anxiety in the long run. Negative, 'safety-seeking' behaviours are really attempts to fool the self into thinking that one is coping. Panic patients often sit down, for example, to avoid getting the expected (but hardly possible) heart attack – doing this, however, keeps alive the belief that they might have died, because they have failed to give themselves the chance to disprove that belief. We can see, however, that even the smallest possibility of death is such an extreme threat that it can easily be seen as rational to avoid any chance of it. Other safety behaviours described by Beck and Emery (1985) are excessive smoking, drinking and even masturbation.

One aspect of avoidant behaviour that Beck and Emery (1985) bring out well is its adverse effects on interpersonal relationships. Futile self-protective behaviour and complete avoidance of any risk can make one a trying partner. Constant reassurance seeking from partners tends to weary them and probably does not add to the health of the relationship. One client of mine was suffering from social anxiety about her teaching. She kept asking her partner how he thought she had done – a question about which he could say but little because he had not been present. A true aha! moment emerged as she realised the futility of this ploy and then rapidly overcame the difficulty by 'dropping the safety behaviour' of reassurance seeking – the closest to a single-session 'cure' that I have ever witnessed.

Reassurance seeking is likely to be a pattern that the client repeats with the therapist. It can seem rather harsh to refuse any reassurance, so perhaps 'the tone to strive for is limited and regretful reassurance' (Wills, 2008, p. 104).

Beck's early anxiety formulations led to great progress in treating anxiety, especially those for panic disorder by the Beck-influenced researchers, David Barlow, David Clark, Paul Salkovskis and Adrian Wells. 'Catastrophic thinking', identified in such thoughts as 'I will die from a heart attack' and 'I am going mad', were clearly evident in many panic clients. Researchers were, however, puzzled by the fact that when clients did not actually die or go mad they did not then consider their beliefs disconfirmed. This eventually appeared to be explained by a range of behaviours that played crucial roles in the maintenance of the disorder. Avoidance, for example, meant that the sufferer continued to avoid situations where the panic reaction might be triggered. Although this is an understandable human response, it inhibited the client from finding out that he was actually very unlikely to have to endure the catastrophes that his 'misinterpretations' suggested could happen.

Many clients will be hyper-vigilant for every little sign that there could be a problem. Blood-phobic clients show an almost superhuman ability to spot tiny quantities of the colour red at great distances (Rachman, 1997a). Such vigilance is bound to increase the amount of threat detected and will tend to ratchet up the feeling of anxiety. Clients with anxiety also develop ways of seeking reassurance about their anxieties from other people.

Classically, the person with health anxiety will seek many consultations from doctors because each one never quite gives complete reassurance.

Reassurance seeking is really one of many forms of 'safety-seeking behaviour' strategies (Salkovskis, 1996a). These are strategies which the client believes she has to engage with to keep 'safe' – though in many situations the degree of danger will have been exaggerated and therefore the search for safety is redundant. For example, a client experiencing social anxiety about being thought stupid might adopt highly academic language. This may only result in other people having a different set of negative views about him. This powerful explanatory notion has since been detected in many other areas of psychological problems. Salkovskis (1996a, p. 72) offers the anxiety formula to explain the 'resonance or interlock (that) is set up between beliefs concerning threat and the way the person responds to that perceived threat':

$$\text{Anxiety} = \frac{\text{Perceived probability of threat} \times \text{Perceived cost/awfulness of danger}}{\text{Perceived ability to cope with danger} + \text{Perceived 'rescue factors'}}$$

Safety behaviours can be seen as strategies to reduce the sum above the line and increase the sum below the line – to minimise the resulting anxiety score. Once in anxiety mode, the person will tend towards over-vigilance against danger and towards being over-controlling of their behaviour – setting up the interlock and all within the context of ongoing cognitive distortion. Clients suffering from intrusive obsessions often fear doing the thing that is most unlike them – 'ego dystonic' in the jargon. They also seem to have meta-cognitive beliefs that they can avoid doing these negative things only by severely suppressing and neutralising their obsessive thoughts, often employing rituals to help them do this (Wells, 1997). The negative cognitive theme seems to be one of an overly conscientious concept of responsibility – 'any form of control equals responsibility for outcome', as Salkovskis (1996a, p. 58) puts it.

A recent helpful addition to understanding the omnipresence of safety behaviours in a key problem area has come from Harvey's (2002) model of insomnia – a very frequent problem with clients. One of my clients revealed the following complex reaction to feeling anxious on waking: 'I feel bad' → 'It must be because I didn't sleep for 8 hours' → 'I will stay in bed' (several hours later) → 'I still feel bad, I'd better have a shower' (after very long shower) → 'Oh no, I still feel bad, I must have really lost it this time.' Such reactions have a strong potential to maintain both anxiety and sleeping problems.

Salkovskis (1996a, p. 72) sees the new types of cognitive therapy that have evolved by using these new formulations to reroute such negative patterns as nevertheless 'part of the legacy of Aaron T. Beck: a flexible, empirically based view of emotions uniquely normalising and emphasising empowerment'.

11

Strategies that address negative attention bias strengthen the cognitive therapy model

The focus of cognitive therapy on content of problematic cognitive functioning seemed to lead naturally to the practice of trying to change or modify that content. This practice had to work as an experimental project, for it did not necessarily follow that changing content of negative thoughts would necessarily change accompanying emotions and behaviours. Some have argued, for example, that the negative thoughts are just 'epiphenomena' – merely coincidental factors with no causal role. There is now, however, evidence of such a causal effect: for example, the role of 'catastrophic misinterpretations' in panic symptoms (Clark, 1996).

It is, however, now clear to CBT therapists that content alone does not explain the effect of negative cognition in psychopathology, nor does modifying such content always elicit change. Dryden (1995), for example, helpfully clarifies that intellectual insight usually does precede emotional and deeper philosophical insight. It can be helpful for therapists to be aware of this, as clients not infrequently say, 'I know rationally that I am not unlovable, but I still *feel* that I am.' Clients typically need a period of 'trying on' and 'working through' new beliefs.

Recent developments in CBT suggest that decentring (Safran & Segal, 1990) and distancing (Beck, 1976) from negative thoughts are connected to the degree of attention that people give to them. Many people seem to have negative thoughts identical to those that disturb sufferers but are able to 'shrug them off' without engaging with them. What distinguishes sufferers is that they engage with these negative thoughts in a more fixated way. Such problem areas typically include obsession, compulsions and worries, and they are characterised by intrusive and perseverative ruminations – thinking too much and paying too much attention to thoughts. Rachman and da Silva (1978), for example, revealed that most people have obsessive thoughts at times, though relatively few are drawn into obsessive engagement with the thoughts. Similar processes seem to work in the worry content connected with GAD (general anxiety disorder) thoughts (Wells, 1997, 2000). Recognising the role of problems of attention is important because therapists will often need to address the negative effects of such attention with some countermeasures in therapy.

Beck now shares this view (Alford & Beck, 1997), but the question is whether the current CT/CBT view was already apparent in his earlier works. Beck has often suggested that the seeds of most of his ideas were sown in his work in the 1960s. We turn to these works to examine what they say about attention and then link them to later work.

In the papers 'Thinking and depression', parts I (1963) and II (1964), Beck uses the term 'processes', but his main emphasis is on distortion. Yet he also refers to what would now be termed 'attentional processes':

Negative thoughts . . . were also observed in the patients' ruminations or 'free associations'. . . . The severely depressed patients often experienced uninterrupted sequences of depressed associations, completely independent of the external situation.

(Beck, 1963, p. 326)

It is interesting to note the parallel between depressive rumination and free association, raising the possibility that certain styles of therapeutic exploration might enhance depression – an experience sometimes reported by clients describing experiences of other types of therapy. It could be that clients who persist with this type of therapy do indeed have a 'need to suffer'!

Beck (1963) uses the term 'perseveration' to refer to problems of attention. The whole cognitive organisation influences psychopathology through distorted thoughts considered in repetitive fashion:

> In addition, those idiosyncratic cognitions tended to occur repetitively in the patient's ruminations and stream of associations.
>
> (Beck, 1963, p. 330)

In an early description of the schema concept, Beck (1964, p. 563) suggests that schemas influence attention bias:

> Schemas not only pattern the cognitive responses . . . but to some extent channel the stream of associations and ruminations as well.

Clients with OCD (Wells, 1997) and GAD (Leahy, 2005) have the same thoughts as non-sufferers but pay a different type of attention to them, and Beck (1964) made similar observations about depressed clients:

> The typical thoughts of depressed patients . . . are not that different from the notions that normal people occasionally entertain and then dismiss. . . . Why does the depressed patient appear to cling to his painful ideas in the face of contradictory evidence?
>
> (Beck, 1964, p. 566)

The answer is that the ideas are empowered by potent schematic beliefs operating a 'compelling grip' on the client:

The depressed individual will be affected by the idea with the greatest intensity rather than the greatest 'truth value'.

(Beck, 1964, p. 566)

This suggests more sophisticated thinking than the supposedly 'veridical' (only accurately 'true' thoughts are 'healthy') model of early CBT.

Beck (1964) gives some brief description of therapy based on these ideas about psychopathology – with cognitive processes again referred to in parallel with other therapist activities. Clients are 'prone to perseverate on a few interpretations of the situation' (Beck, 1964, p. 568), so therapists aim to widen the view to other perspectives. Therapists may have to be both creative and structured because the patient 'is apt to be distracted by the relentlessness of depressive cognitions. The compelling quality of the depressive cognitions may be so strong as to make any form of insight psychotherapy fruitless' (Beck, 1964, pp. 568–569).

Kovacs and Beck (1978, pp. 525–526) indicate that cognition in psychopathology is broader than just content:

Cognition is a broad term that refers to both the content of thought and the processes involved in thinking. Ways of perceiving and processing material, the mechanisms and content of memory and recall, and problems solving attitudes and strategies are all aspects of cognition. In short, cognition encompasses the processes of knowing as well as the products of knowing.

The importance of cognitive processes, especially attention, became clearer as Beck worked on anxiety disorders. Salkovskis (1996a) notes that Beck's theory of anxiety had three main elements: selective attention to feared objects, physiological change, and, changes in behaviour. Selective attention means that anxious clients are more sensitive to signs of possible threat – partly an automatic reaction but also one that involves deliberate scanning for danger signals. The more danger signals are looked for, the more they are seen when present and 'seen' when not present.

Beck et al. (1974a, p. 324) describe the problem of attention:

The anxiety prone . . . patient differs from the normal in that . . . he systematically misconstrues innocuous situations as dangerous . . . and *perseveres* in having thoughts or visual images about being physically or psychologically injured. (*italics added*)

Perseveration has become part of the formulation of anxiety, according to Beck and Emery (1985, p. 31):

The anxious person . . . is 'bound' to stimuli perceived as threatening . . . is hyper-vigilant, constantly scanning the environment for signs of impending disaster.

For cognitive treatment of anxiety, Beck and Emery (1985) add interventions to shift the attention paid to anxious thoughts, especially developing more awareness and acceptance of anxious feeling. Developing self-monitoring can help the anxious client gain distance from his anxiogenic thinking. Clients may also develop a more helpful and reflective stance towards underlying negative thoughts so that they can answer the question, 'What is it that I am really afraid of here?' The acceptance of anxious feelings is the first step of managing them in Beck and Emery's (1985) A-W-A-R-E strategy:

Accept the anxious feelings.
Watch the anxious feelings move around your body and mind.[1]
Act with anxiety.
Repeat steps 1–3 over.
Expect the best to happen.

Processes of attention have been increasingly targeted in cognitive approaches to anxiety. Wells and Mathews (1994) developed a major framework for tracing the relationship between processes of attention and different emotional disorders. Wells (1997, 2000) has drawn up problem formulations that explicitly include attentional and self-attentional processes for specific disorders.

In social anxiety, for example, self-directed attention plays a crucial role in symptom maintenance. For example, in social situations, clients increasingly focus on their own sense of embarrassment. Clients have strong internal images during which they imagine other people looking critically at them – blushing, for example. CB therapy therefore increasingly encourages clients with social anxiety to look outwards from themselves at the thing they fear and avoid most: how people are *actually* paying attention to them. People *may* be critical but more often the evidence is benign – useful disconfirmation of such fears (Wells, 1997). If clients are being criticised, however, it is better for them to know this so they can develop counter-strategies.

Attention to negative phenomena was described in Beck's early writings and is now right at the cutting edge of the development of cognitive therapy.

Note

1 NB: watching should be non-judgemental – 'neither good nor bad'.

12

Meta-cognition – the way people think about thinking – also influences the way they feel and behave

> Although the notion of 'distancing' has been a central concept within cognitive clinical theory for some time (Beck, 1976, pp. 242–245), the relationship between clinical construct and cognitive science has not previously been explicated. . . . Distancing is an active, regulatory process that involves the activation of the meta-cognitive level of functioning.
>
> (Alford & Beck, 1997, p. 65)

Meta-cognition – the ability both to think about our thinking and to apply cognitive processes, such as memory and attention, to our thinking – is one of the highest levels of thought. Human beings unquestionably do think – and spend much of their waking hours doing so. We think about our thinking for better or worse. Reflective thinking, for example, helps us to gain 'distance' from and override our negative thoughts – the first step in cognitive restructuring. Because we are FFHBs[1] (Dryden, 1991), however, we inevitably sometimes mess up thinking about our thinking and develop a form of meta-cognition that only digs us deeper into the mire of psychopathology (Wells, 1997, 2000; Papageorgiou & Wells, 2003).

Because the rise of cognitive therapy coincided with the 'cognitive revolution' in general psychology, it is often assumed that the two phenomena must be strongly related. In fact, they were not, as Beck's above quotation acknowledges, there was little overlap in the early years, though there has been considerable catch-up in more recent times. Beck's initial work developed almost entirely within a clinical context and followed its own particular line of epistemology (Point 14). British research psychologists such as Teasdale and Wells have made particularly noteworthy contributions in supplying more purely psychological content to CBT formulations, especially in the area of meta-cognition. As we might also expect, however, the advent of research psychologists in the field has also increased the incidence of barely penetrable language and papers (one of the clearest correlations known to science!).

Beck's early writings contain many passages that imply that he well understood the more subtle cognitive processes involved in psychopathology, as Point 11 on the role of attention shows. He was concerned, however, to develop an effective way of helping in areas characterised by urgent need and did not always have time to add the bedevilling detail so loved by academics. To some extent, the finer detail was subsumed in the overriding schema concept. We noted earlier that Wells' (2000) review of Beck's schema concept shows that it is based on the idea of a schema as a structure that both contains cognitive content and organises cognitive processes. While cognitive processes are clearly implied in Beck's early work, a clearer description was given of cognitive content, especially assumptions and beliefs. Alford and Beck (1997, p. 1), however, stress the importance of the whole cognitive organisation and fear that distinguishing between 'polar' concepts of content and process might lay cognitive therapy open to the problems of 'dualism'. They prefer to emphasise that cognitive therapy has a 'multidimensional nature' (p. 3).

As Beck re-engaged with research on schizophrenia, he realised that meta-cognition plays a key role in its maintenance, Alford and Beck (1997) offer an illustrative example of working with a client with a paranoid delusion. The patient has established some distance from his belief about persecution but is now faced with a dilemma: if he acknowledges that there is no conspiracy, the implication to him is that there must be something wrong with *him* – a more threatening possibility than the existence of a conspiracy. Here, then, we are back at the oldest of psychotherapeutic terms – 'insight'. Beck's work on schizophrenia has offered a more thorough-going understanding of what insight is and, as we might expect, he has developed a scale to measure and delineate its depth and shape, the Beck Cognitive Insight Scale (Beck et al., 2004).

Interestingly, it has been left to others to develop the more explicit nature of meta-cognitive processes in the fields of Beck's original research – anxiety and depression. The basic thrust of Wells' work has been to give clearer descriptions and cognitive accounts of all the wider processing phenomena in the generation of psychopathology. He has particularly focused on the anxiety disorders and has shown that

> In summary, research on attentional bias in anxiety demonstrates a reliable bias effect across a range of paradigms and a range of anxiety disorders. The attention data are consistent with predictions based on Beck's general theory of anxiety disorder. Individuals with anxiety show attentional bias for schema congruent danger information. Nevertheless, the underlying mechanisms for bias effects require systematic evaluation.
>
> (Wells, 1997, p. 13)

Wells' work on attention has been part of work that contributes to our understanding of the broader field of meta-cognition. He has, for example, revealed that one of the factors that maintains the mechanisms of worry in GAD sufferers (for whom worry is usually the central problem) is that people have positive beliefs about worry – *Worrying helps me remember things.* As noted in our earlier section on evolutionary mechanisms, this particular belief has a kernel of truth, but it is nearly always helpful to get clients to review the nature and range of these beliefs, as they tend to contain dysfunctional elements.

Wells (2000) has helpfully shown that there are two types of worry at work in GAD: type 1 focuses on external events, whereas type 2 worry is meta-cognitive. Type 2 worry may be 'positive' – 'If I worry a lot about this, I will find a solution' (quite close to one of Ellis' irrational beliefs) – or 'negative' – 'Worrying like this will make me go mad.' Thus, different worry strategies may develop and interact with each other. Wells' work (1997, 2000) offers help on identifying negative meta-cognitive strategies in client discourse (and using measures[2]) and on therapeutic work designed to modify them.

Before leaving this Point, we should also make some mention of another cognitive process – memory. Kovacs and Beck (1978) note that 'in the absence of a comprehensive theory of memory' the schema concept helps to explain both the consistencies in people's reactions to events and the differences in the way different people respond to the same events. Schemas allow people to screen, code and assess the full range of internal and external stimuli. Beck's (1967; Beck et al., 1979b) books on depression remain classic texts to this day. These texts describe how his research into the cognitive functioning of depressed clients led directly into his model of cognitive therapy. The 'negative attentional bias' in attention and memory was shown to reinforce the maintenance of depression and was therefore a key feature of Beck's model of depression. Williams (1996, p. 105) has suggested that memory in depression becomes subject to 'mnemonic interlock' resulting from traumatic memories. Interlock represents a jamming of memories that then become hazy and are therefore hard to process. Williams (1996, p. 111) therefore goes on to suggest that the 'healing of memory is central to cognitive therapy'. This work has been paralleled by other memory researchers such as Brewin (1996), who has shown the vital role played by negative memories, not only in depression, but also in post-traumatic stress disorder (PTSD).

Beck's contribution here was to develop a wide-ranging model of cognitive organisation, within which many subtle processes were apparent, leaving the space for himself and other researchers to elaborate in the succeeding years.

Notes

1 Fucked up, fallible human beings!
2 See Wells (1997, 2000) for the Metacognitions Questionnaire and the Thought Control Questionnaire.

13

Promoting mindfulness of and mindful attention to negative thoughts is likely to form a major part of cognitive therapy in future

The Points described in the early Part of the book focused very much on the traditional concerns of cognitive therapy, such as negative thoughts, beliefs and schemas. Since Point 10, however, we seem to have been shifting into newer ground and have become familiar with wider concerns connected to the process elements of the client's cognitive organisation. Point 13 is the culmination of these trends and leads us to examine what is increasingly becoming 'the next big thing' in cognitive therapy – mindfulness. Linked as it is with Buddhism, this is creating much excitement in the field. In order to assess its significance, we will need to look quite carefully at what is being claimed on its behalf. We will begin by examining its basis in previous theory. We will find, however, that several different – not entirely harmonious – elements emerge. This will lead us to a final consideration of two points:

- Are all mindfulness exponents talking about the same thing?
- Is it really part of cognitive therapy?

Mindfulness – which might be defined as 'using awareness and thoughts to bring consciousness fully into the present moment' – is best known as an ancient meditation practice, particularly associated with Buddhism. It has achieved some recognition in Western societies both through popular Buddhist groups and literature such as the books by Thich Nhat Hahn.

The link between early Beckian theory and mindfulness focuses on the concept of 'distancing' – first fully espoused by Beck (1976, pp. 242–245). Interestingly, Beck is said to be a regular meditater, and in 2005, wrote an interesting article on 'Buddhism and Cognitive Therapy' prior to a well-publicised meeting with the Dalai Lama (Beck, 2005b). In the article he compares Buddhism's and cognitive therapy's common aim of eliminating mental afflictions through mental training. He describes three main cognitive therapy strategies – a sequence of distancing, reframing and decentring. Decentring that has been successful allows a reorientation of patterns of thinking, similar to the processes of mindfulness meditation. The person's concerns become less exaggerated and self-referent, allowing for more compassion and empathy for the self and for others.

Beck here describes certain allied developments in cognitive therapy – namely the intentional refocusing of attention in social phobia described by Clark and Ehlers and the more effortful attentional training package, developed by Wells (2000). The package has been shown to be helpful for both clients with panic symptoms and depressed clients (Papageorgiou & Wells, 2003; Wells, 2000). Beck sees these developments as

> reasonably conceived within the cognitive model, since they are based on the theory of overinvestment in unhelpful (dysfunctional) ideas and use a specialised cognitive technique to attenuate them. Conceptually, the techniques enhance executive functioning so that attentional resources can be redeployed. . . . The procedure of effortful focusing is comparable to a form of Buddhist meditation known as 'one point concentration'.
>
> (Beck, 2005b, p. 3)

Mindfulness-based cognitive therapy (MBCT) has also been advocated as a new model of relapse prevention in depression (Segal et al., 2002) and is built on a fusion of more traditional cognitive therapy and ideas of a more meditation-based nature taken from the 'mindfulness' model of Jon Kabat-Zinn (2001), the latter being the predominant component. Mindfulness has also been assimilated into both dialetical behaviour therapy (DBT) (Linehan, 1993) and acceptance and commitment therapy (ACT) (Hayes et al., 2004). Whereas the procedures of Wells, Clark and Ehlers can all be incorporated into one on one therapy sessions, some aspects of the mindfulness work in MBCT and ACT depend on regular group meetings, in some ways resembling yoga courses. Additionally, they require ongoing mindfulness practice by therapists running programmes. Beck (2005b, p. 3) sees some distancing from cognitive therapy in these programmes:

> The proponents of the mindfulness strategies as utilized in Mindfulness-based CT, Dialetical Behavior Therapy and Acceptance and Commitment Therapy explicitly differentiate their approach from CT and its emphasis on cognitive restructuring of dysfunctional cognitions.

I detect some reservation in these comments and in some other comments by Judith Beck, implying that a passive, even if 'mindful' approach to depressogenic symptoms could accentuate them.

In summary, mindfulness has clearly become a hot topic in cognitive therapy, but I would say that there is some confusion about what exactly it means, how it relates to established theory, and how it is best pursued. Given the empirical bent of most cognitive therapists, I would expect that these questions will be clarified in the coming years.

In terms of the larger narrative of this part of the book, I have commented on how Beck has generally been pleased to positively acknowledge the way people have developed his ideas. This denotes a welcome lack of control freakery in a field where that has been displayed by other 'guardians of the truth' in therapy. Sometimes I have been surprised by Beck's rather benign approach to some offshoots, so it is quite nice here to detect at last some reservation! Suffice it to say just that for now, but a deeper consideration of Beck as the 'leader' of a therapeutic movement will form part of the conclusion to this book.

14

Beckian epistemology has a clear process for developing appropriate therapeutic knowledge for cognitive therapists to follow

> Beck's career models the exponential effectiveness of working equally hard in the areas of conceptualisation, empirical research and therapy applications. His discoveries and innovations in each area are enhanced by knowledge gained in the other two areas. . . . For example, beginning with the 1959 paper on dream content of depressed patients (Beck & Hurvich, 1959), his empirical work in the area of depression *preceded* development of his cognitive theory of depression, first published in 1967. His therapy, so familiar to us today, developed over the next 15 years; principles of that therapy protocol were first published between 1974 and 1979.
>
> (Padesky, 2004, p. 12)

David M. Clark (1996) describes the evolution of his model of panic disorder. This model has been hailed as an exemplar of clear, research-based and empirically tested model building: not only of the causes but also of the treatment of panic. Clark explains how he built his approach on the research model developed by Beck, firstly, in his research on depression and then later in other areas. This research model has undoubtedly been influential in increasing rigour in psychotherapy research. It has also been characterised by a strong ethical concern not to make claims for any form of treatment before efficacy research has shown it to be effective.

D. M. Clark (1996) describes the characteristic processes by which Beck's cognitive therapy has developed comprehensive approaches to models of psychopathology. He locates the development of cognitive behavioural models – specific models particular to specific disorders – in the early steps of Beck's work on depression. The process has been refined somewhat as CBT has expanded in terms of the numbers of practitioners and researchers involved in the multifarious treatment areas in which it is now participating. Clark describes the process as having five characteristic stages:

1 moving from clinical insight to specify a simple clinical model for a particular problem area
2 experimental investigation of the model
3 detailed accounts of factors that prevent cognitive change in the absence of treatment
4 carefully chosen treatment procedures for targeting cognitive change
5 controlled trials of the effectiveness of those procedures.

Clark (1996) is able to show how he and others moved through these various stages to develop his cognitive model of panic disorder, developing, firstly, quite subtle experimental tests of the basic psychological constructs. Only when these were tested and established could the theoretical model be launched. Once the theoretical model was established, testing could begin on possible interventions. Interventions were first tested as stand-alone trials because it would be premature to deliver them as part of a whole therapeutic package. As likely interventions began to shape up, overall protocols could be developed and tested.

This process was essentially forged from Beck's often solo work on developing the cognitive therapy of depression. It has served the development of cognitive therapy and CBT as a good template and has been vital in winning the confidence of necessary outside allies such as practice and funding agencies in raising the credibility of the model.

A noteworthy feature of the whole process is the tight fit between each step and the way the steps build up mutual interaction of cognitive therapy theory and practice:

In science, the direction a discipline takes is determined by the conduct of systematic observations; however, these observations themselves are in turn products of the theoretical perspectives of scientists within a given cultural context.

(Alford & Beck, 1997, p. 5)

The protocol has played a noteworthy role in building the fit between theory and practice in cognitive therapy. The final Point will be on the cognitive therapy skills protocol and will mark a good way to end this part of the book and to lead us into the next part on practice.

15

Protocol development and the specification of skills have proved important factors in linking CBT theory and practice

> The system of psychotherapeutic techniques is clearly and explicitly defined in our cognitive therapy treatment manuals, especially in the manual on the treatment of depression. The uniformity of treatment procedures has been confirmed by monitoring the interviews (by means of tape recordings of the psychotherapists who have participated in our training research program.
>
> (Beck, 1976, p. 332)

The linkage of skills and process is achieved only vaguely in some models of therapeutic practice. The cognitive tradition has been towards explicitness and specificity. Carl Rogers, however, led the way by using recordings to explore therapist behaviour:

> I remember the excitement of gathering round the tape recorder to listen and learn what happened when such and such an intervention was used. We learnt a lot from that.
>
> (Rogers, 1980, p. 127)

Tapes of therapy sessions were also used by Ellis. Tapes have many uses for training purposes, as they allow the monitoring of skill use. Identifying precise skills meant that they could be written up into protocols. Beck wrote up a treatment manual for use in the University of Pennsylvania's early trials of the cognitive therapy of depression. Outlines appeared in the 1976 book and were then written up more fully in the Beck et al. (1979b) book. The 1979b book is surprisingly stylishly written given that it began life as a protocol. Perhaps, however, it still did give a feeling of 'prescription' that sticks in the throat of some therapists and trainees and may have given rise to some of the resistance to CBT (Sanders & Wills, 2005; Wills, 2008). There has been much debate on protocols: on the whole, they probably do work, but there may be more need for flexibility – or at least the degree of potentially helpful flexibility needs to be explored and defined (Dobson & Shaw, 1993). There may also be elements of therapeutic treatment that cannot easily be put into a protocol – for example, how to maintain the therapy relationship and how to exercise clinical judgement. Dobson and Shaw (1993) also suggest that formulation making may fall somewhere between the technique and relationship learning. These matters will be further discussed in Part 2, alongside descriptions of attempts to define and measure proficiency in cognitive therapy skills and practice.

Conclusion to Part 1

A consideration of Beck's ideas about therapeutic theory reveals them as wide-ranging and profound. As a man of ideas, he shows himself to be eclectic and pragmatic. At a time of deadening specialism in academic fields, he is an open and free spirit. Briefly considering comparison with other comparable figures, he might be said to have been more open than Freud. Though he has fought his corner, he has been more open and responsive to criticism. He has been more rigorous and persistent in his empirical work than Rogers and Ellis, and has shown more diplomatic skill than either. The closest comparison to my mind is with Darwin. Darwin's theory is probably even more parsimonious and yet more elegant than Beck's and therefore tops them all. Beck shared Darwin's early physical frailty but perhaps was more robust in overcoming it. His theory has mighty enemies, as did that of Darwin, and he has shown more courage in putting it in the public domain than Darwin did. He is a gentle and nice person – and yet, like Darwin, he has a touch of steel when needed. While Darwin's theory has profoundly shaped much modern science and thought, Beck's theories have had more practical effects in relieving mental suffering – but to see this more clearly, we need to proceed to Part 2.

Part 2

PRACTICE

Beck's cognitive therapy – a principled model: 15 Points about the practice model

The cognitive therapy model developed by Aaron and Judith Beck has been characterised by its parsimony, clarity and highly integrated nature. Beck has described himself as a 'pragmatist', ready to gather helpful aspects of therapy from a wider range of sources. Yet the ideas thus gathered are only included in so far as they explain and/or help change problems and fit within the overall framework of the model. Beck laid out the first few points of description of the model in his papers in the early 1960s. These were extended into some principles of treatment in the 1976 and 1979 books. They were more explicitly codified into principle statements and expanded upon in Beck and Emery (1985) and revised somewhat in Judith's 1995 book (Beck, 1995). This is a thoroughly Beckian approach: a simple set of axiomatic principles have slowly evolved along with learning from the experience of process and outcomes of the therapy but have also been subtly adapted to new findings and feedback from the therapy world. Because these principles map so well onto practice skills, we will review them and use them as a template for describing 15 main Points of the practice section of this book. We begin by stating the version of the 11 principles given by Judith Beck (1995):

a   Cognitive therapy is based on an ever-evolving formulation of the client and her problem in cognitive terms.

b   Cognitive therapy requires a sound therapeutic relationship.

c   Cognitive therapy emphasises collaboration and active participation.

d   Cognitive therapy aims to be time-limited.

e   Cognitive therapy sessions are structured and directional.

f   Cognitive therapy is goal orientated and problem focused.

g   Cognitive therapy initially emphasises the present.

h   Cognitive therapy is educative, aims to teach the client to be her own therapist, and emphasises relapse prevention.[1]

i   Homework is a central feature of cognitive therapy.

j   Cognitive therapy aims to teach clients to identify, evaluate and respond to their dysfunctional thoughts and beliefs.

k   Cognitive therapy uses a variety of techniques to change thinking, mood and behaviour.

Wills (2008) explains how these cognitive therapy principles can be grouped to describe its conceptual base (principle a), its relationship base (principles b and c), the main strategic aspects of cognitive therapy (principles d to h), and its skills base (principles i to k). The principles will be expanded to generate the 15 Points for this part of the book. Four extra Points will be added: one to the conceptual base to distinguish between using the formulation to focus interventions and using it to track interpersonal issues in therapy. Two extra Points will be added to the skills base section to give wider expression to the wealth of techniques in cognitive therapy. A final fifteenth Point will be added to cover Beck's contribution to the development of measures for assessing therapeutic skill learning. This will describe the development and evolution of the Cognitive Therapy Scale (Milne et al., 2001; Young & Beck, 1980, 1988). The scale and the accompanying manual on its use are invaluable resources to cognitive therapists and are available as downloads on Beck's Academy of Cognitive Therapy website.

The manual has many useful insights and these will be referred to throughout this section.

In the final dozen pages of his masterwork on depression, Beck (1967) sketched out how he thought a cognitive model (note lower-case 'c') could work, especially connoting the importance of identifying and testing negative beliefs that seemed to maintain the depression. These notes were expanded in *Cognitive Therapy and the Emotional Disorders* (Beck, 1976) to three chapters on cognitive therapy's principles, techniques and application to depression, respectively. Beck and his research team expanded his ideas on treatment to 30, then 70 and then 160 pages of manual before turning them into a 396-page classic and revolutionary text, *Cognitive Therapy of Depression* (Beck et al., 1979b). The following Points will pay particularly close attention to early descriptions, updated with the more recent thoughts of both Beck and his wider group.

Note

1 Judith uses the term 'patient'. I have preferred the more usual British usage of 'client'.

16

Cognitive therapists use formulation to focus therapeutic work

> Titus [Roman general in charge of the siege of Jerusalem] was furiously angry. . . . He reminded . . . [his undisciplined soldiers] . . . that . . . for Romans, even victory, without discipline is dishonourable.
>
> (Furneaux, 1973, p. 136)

Young and Beck (1980, p. 13) stress the fact that an effective cognitive therapist should be formulating all the time as she collects cognitive data: 'The therapist is like a detective who has a lot of clues but has still not solved the crime.' As the cognitive clues are fitted together, it should slowly become clear what the target areas are and, even, what might be the best ways of addressing them. Without an overall formulation, targeting areas would be hit or miss, and progress would be erratic and, like the victories of Titus' undisciplined soldiers, 'dishonourable'! Indeed, as we shall see when we explore the use of the Cognitive Therapy Scale (CTS), cognitive therapy raters are strongly advised to separate rating the quality of interventions from whether change actually seems to occur as a result of them, because 'Sometimes a therapist will apply techniques very skilfully, yet a particular patient may be extremely rigid or unyielding and does not respond' (Young & Beck, 1980, p. 22).

The theoretical importance of formulation was stressed in Part 1. Formulations are helpful not only in guiding an understanding of the client's situation but also in guiding how therapeutic work should be aimed by targeting key elements of the formulation. In Point 1, we noted that Persons (1989) offered some very clear guidance on using formulations in practice, and we will use her points as a template for tracking Point 17. Point 16 will be focused on using the content of formulations to understand the relationship between clients' various symptoms and problems, choosing starting points and methods for treatment, and monitoring client reactions to these choices. Point 17 will cover the same ground in relation to the more interpersonal and covert processes in therapy. Both Points will be illustrated by offering typical formulations.

Beck et al.'s (1979b) formulation of depression showed how the client's cognitive organisation plays a key role at the centre of the various mental and physical systems generating the symptoms of depression. The behavioural reaction of withdrawal, for example, could be underpinned by a series of cognitions such as 'I don't enjoy going out anymore', 'People do not want to meet me when I am like this', and 'There's no point in trying to make things better' – all of which would tend to keep the client in withdrawal mode. Staying in the withdrawn position will have a number of important consequences for the depressed person. Firstly, the client is not likely to encounter experiences that might disconfirm her negative thoughts and beliefs. Secondly, staying in the withdrawn position is likely to lead to the client following a way of life predicated on low levels of activity and greater lethargy. Thirdly, because the client is not going out to meet the world, the world may well after a time stop coming to meet her – especially if her company is relatively 'unrewarding'. As the client becomes more and more isolated, she will spend longer and longer periods of time by herself, during which, because she is in a depressed mood, she will be highly likely to be prone to negative rumination. The more time she spends ruminating, the lower her mood will become and the lower her mood, the more time she will spend ruminating.[1] The time spent ruminating may be enhanced by poor sleep quality and quantity. A vicious cycle drawn to formulate the factors described above in abbreviated form is shown in Figure 4.

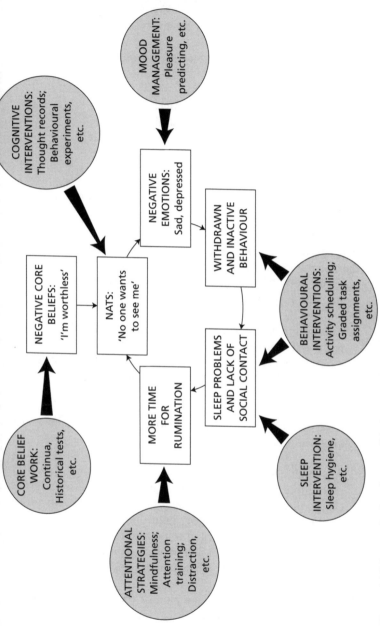

Figure 4 Vicious cycle showing possible intervention points

The formulation map shows the various possible intervention points:

Symptom focus:	Intervention:
Withdrawn behaviour:	Behavioural activation
Negative predictions:	Behavioural experiment
Negative thoughts:	Cognitive restructuring
Cognitive ruminations:	Attentional strategies
Sleep problems:	Sleep intervention (Espie, 2006)
Negative schemas:	Core belief work (Greenberger & Padesky, 1995)

Any or all of these strategies could be starting points for therapeutic work. To decide between them, we need to use the skills of both 'clinical judgement' and 'client-sensitive judgement'. The first (nomothetic formulation) is illustrated below:

For example, if the client is very depressed, this probably rules out cognitive interventions initially at least. Behavioural interventions are likely the best bet and may well lead to both emotional and physiological relief – running counter to the effects of lethargy.

But we may also need 'client-sensitive judgement skills' (idiographic formulation):

Although this client is very depressed, she is also very preoccupied by the recent death of her father – with whom she claims there is much 'unfinished business'. As the therapist tried to steer therapy to more immediate concerns, the client says, 'No one wants to listen to me about this.' It is apparent then that no intervention that we use can just proceed without taking some cognizance of this preoccupation.

Persons (2005) has been a champion of the idiographic formulation and believes that only this can improve the effectiveness of therapy in the long run. It is, she says, the 'dirty little secret' (Persons, 2005, p. 107) of cognitive therapy that if we ever used the treatment protocols as they were written, 'we'd get lousy adherence scores' (Persons, 2005, p. 107).

Beck has given us templates for both generic and individual formulation – how and when we should combine these methods is part of the unfolding art of cognitive practice.

Note

1 I notice that at this point even my writing has taken on the style of a 'vicious cycle'.

17

Cognitive therapists, like other therapists, use formulation to tackle interpersonal and alliance issues

> I may do or say something that is hurtful, rejecting or insulting to the patient . . . the client will need to tell this to the therapist . . . such reports are extremely valuable in giving us information that will help the therapy. In fact these reports are often the most valuable material that we obtain in treatment.
>
> (Adapted from Beck et al., 1979b, p. 82)

Formulations can also be used to deal with interpersonal issues that arise in therapy, often by reference to the interpersonal beliefs explicit or implicit in the formulation. For example, a client may believe that 'People do not care about me.' Such a client may give up on the therapist or the therapy because of this belief and not attend a scheduled session. The therapist might decide that the best way to disconfirm his belief would be to contact him and encourage him to come back into therapy. If the formulation showed him as believing that 'People interfere with me and don't let me make my own decisions', the therapist may reject such a course of action.

Interpersonal work becomes more crucial when working with clients' negative personality patterns. The diagnostic label 'personality disorder' has, for good reasons, proved controversial. Controversy has partly been fuelled by a misunderstanding of the term based on its associations with dangerousness and/or criminality. Only a small part of even the official spectrum of personality disorders, however, concerns such issues. The present author feels some unease about the way this problem has been dealt with in CBT and prefers the term 'personality pattern'. He also regards personality problems as being more pervasive and 'normal' in everyday therapy work than is sometimes realised. Beck, however, has made a striking and destigmatising contribution to the treatment of such problems. He has suggested that, rather like more 'ordinary' psychological problems, such personality patterns may be linked to evolutionary survival patterns. These have specific and distinct cognitive profiles that can be engaged with in essentially similar ways as in standard cognitive therapy. Such work, however, is usually more long term and relies heavily on interpersonally skilled use of the therapeutic relationship (Beck, Freeman & Associates, 2004).

The key skills in dealing with such problems involve a series of clinical judgements: discerning problematic situations, deciding whether to act on them, and then formulating a therapeutic response. It is often wise to delay over-ready reaction and take the issue to supervision. A rule of thumb of waiting until some pattern has shown itself three times may be useful. It is also useful to reflect on our own behaviour and consider whether we have been consciously or unconsciously provocative. It would be a rare therapist who did not have buttons that got pushed sometimes.

It is, however, sometimes desirable and necessary to react in the moment, and then the therapist must cultivate the skill of immediacy (Wills, 2008). This involves the therapist telling the client in a non-threatening way how she is experiencing him at that moment, and then inviting an open discussion and reflection on what is 'happening between us'. Although this sounds quite threatening, clients are often all too aware of how people experience them, and it can be a relief for the therapist to bring it out into the open. At worst, these confrontations can get messy, but at best they often have great breakthrough potential – the therapy ceases to be a 'talking shop' and may become a place that can be experienced as a non-threatening, moment-by-moment experience.

Beck, Freeman and Associates (2004) mainly deal with these types of exchange in relation to working with personality problems, but my own experience is that they occur quite frequently at all levels of therapy. Beck tends to see such situations as being 'driven' by specific core beliefs and inter-personal strategies, and knowing his work in this area can provide a therapist with much help in working productively in them.

18

Cognitive therapy requires a sound therapeutic relationship

The concept of the 'therapeutic relationship' holds a special place in the discourse of psychotherapy. On the one hand, the therapeutic relationship is held to be the chief 'common factor' to all models and to be a decisive, if not *the* decisive determinant, of therapeutic effectiveness (Orlinsky et al., 1994). On the other hand, it is also a term that can be vague in usage, and its importance may be conceptually susceptible to over-inflation (Feltham, 1999).

Beck et al.'s (1979b) description of the therapeutic relationship actually has much in common with that given in the work of Carl Rogers (1957, 1980), though, unlike Rogers, Beck et al. (1979b) regard the 'core conditions' of empathy, warmth and congruence, as necessary, but not sufficient, for change. A collaborative relationship in which the therapist has considerable skill and expertise is regarded as a further necessary factor. From a cognitive theory perspective, one would expect individual clients to react differently to the therapeutic relationship according to their beliefs about relationships. Some clients, for example, may want the therapist to express a lot of empathy, but others might wonder about the sincerity of that same degree of expressed empathy.

In cognitive therapy, client and therapist should ideally form a 'team' that unites and works together to solve the client's key problems (Beck et al., 1979b). To this 'team', the therapist brings a considerable amount of expertise and knowledge about psychological problems and processes of psychological change. This expertise may not, however, prove useful if it cannot be applied to the individual client's life. Clients therefore also bring expertise about their own experiences to the 'team'. Neither client nor therapist can usually succeed alone – success is most likely to come from uniting these two domains of expertise into a working partnership.

Cognitive therapists propose that the 'core conditions' create a relationship within which the therapeutic work takes place. CBT theorists have also pointed out that such relationships are intrinsically rewarding (Sheldon, 1995) and do influence clients (Hudson & Macdonald, 1986). There is also much evidence that CBT therapists seem to be able to combine the skills of giving direction, being empathic and influencing clients as effectively, if not more effectively than, other types of therapists (Keijsers et al., 2000). For CBT work to be effective, however, the therapist needs to have both conceptual and technical expertise as well as interpersonal skills (Padesky & Greenberger, 1995).

Like humanistic therapy, psychodynamic therapy has placed a heavy emphasis on the therapeutic relationship as the vehicle of change – though for rather different reasons. Psychodynamic therapists regard many client problems as being caused or exacerbated by unconscious wishes and motives. They believe that these unconscious wishes will themselves permeate the therapeutic encounter as 'transference reactions'. Transference reactions are, in brief, client responses based on unconscious wishes and may elicit 'counter-transference' from the therapist's unconscious. Thus, the therapeutic relationship becomes an arena in which these transference and counter-transference issues can be 'worked through' and resolved. 'Working through' has been identified as a main activity of psychodynamic therapy (Holmes, 2000). As noted in earlier discussion, the activity of 'working through' has traditionally been seen as a long-term process, and this factor has therefore identified psychodynamic therapy as being in general a longer-term process than other types of therapy.

In a debate with Albert Ellis in 2000, Beck (www.fenichel.com/Beck-Ellis.shtml; accessed 2/1/09) referred to himself as a 'closet psychoanalyst', though 'critical friend' may perhaps be a better term. While his ideas seem to have taken a similar direction to that of Ellis – away from the 'inefficient' aspects of dynamic therapy – psychoanalytic influences have re-emerged strongly in areas characterised as having the potential for complex relationships, such as the cognitive therapy of personality disorders (Beck, Freeman & Associates, 1990). One way of seeing this is that Beck has encouraged cognitive therapists to be less profligate with time and depth than his erstwhile psychoanalytic colleagues.

19

Cognitive therapists stress the importance of collaboration in the therapeutic relationship

Beck et al. (1979b) defined the therapeutic stance in cognitive therapy as 'collaborative empiricism'. Padesky (2004) suggests that behavioural therapy took an empirical stance towards therapeutic activity. Behavioural empiricism, however, referred only to the behaviour of the therapist. The therapist had set the terms and defined the questions of what had to be found out, and the client was reduced to the position of nearly incidental data collector. It is hard to agree completely with Padesky (2004, p. 7), however, that collaboration can be understood as 'an equal working partnership.' Strictly defined, 'collaboration' merely means 'working together', and people can work together when they see themselves as having quite different roles, even roles with different status. Martin Buber, for example, despite advocating the relevance of an 'I–thou' relationship for therapy, could not agree with Rogers that a relationship where one party seeks unreciprocated help from another can really be 'equal' (Kirschenbaum & Henderson, 1990). It is rare, for a client to match the skills of a well-practised therapist in challenging negative thoughts. Beck and Emery (1985, p. 175) stress the different but interlocking roles:

> The cognitive therapist implies that there is a team approach to the solution of the patient's problem: that is, a therapeutic alliance where the patient supplies raw data (reports on thoughts and behaviour . . .) while the therapist provides structure and expertise on how to solve the problems. The emphasis is on working on problems rather than on

correcting deficits or changing personality. The therapist fosters the attitude 'two heads are better than one' in approaching personal difficulties.

Acknowledging this does not mean that it is helpful for a therapist to adopt a superior position. Beck (1976, p. 221) makes it quite clear that it is unhelpful so to do:

It is useful to conceive of the patient–therapist relationship as a joint effort. It is not the therapist's function to reform the patient: rather his role is working with the patient against 'it', the patient's problem. Placing emphasis on solving problems, rather than his presumed deficits or bad habits, helps the patient to examine his difficulties with more detachment and makes him less prone to experience shame, a sense of inferiority and defensiveness.

The reference to shame here reminds us that various writers, but particularly Gilbert and Andrews (1998), have stressed the importance of this emotion as a frequently occurring factor in therapy.

Cognitive theory itself would imply there is unlikely to be a 'one size fits all' therapeutic relationship, but the Beckian version of therapeutic relationships, which can include direction, structure and education, as well as the traditional values of respect and warmth, appears to offer a wider range of options.

Beck's work offers the principle for working with depressed people that it is usually necessary to address activity levels at the start of therapy. The depressed client often combines a sense of physical lethargy with a sense of hopelessness. To tackle this, it is often helpful for the therapist to be somewhat 'upbeat' in relation to the client. This gives the meta-message that problems can be solved and there is a way of going forward. Being upbeat can, however, be over-applied and the therapist should be ever vigilant for signs of the interpersonal interpretations clients may make of any therapist behaviour.

The following Points – 20 to 24 – are about the strategic base of cognitive therapy. They emphasise the brief, structured and goal-orientated dimensions of cognitive therapy that fit together and are vital because they interact to establish the strategic foundations of the approach. The therapy, for example, has to be structured and goal focused because of the limited time frame. The focused nature of the therapy usually requires that present time dimension of problems is directly addressed first. The directional and structured nature of the process leads into an educational dimension that helps clients better to understand and act on their problems.

20

Cognitive therapy is brief and time-limited

> Just as he [Beck] was completing his analysis, they [Beck and his wife] were attending a meeting of the American Psychoanalytic Association, where they spotted a sign . . . reading '. . . Problems of Re-Analysis.' Beck recalls Phyllis' reaction. 'What!' she exclaimed, 're-analysis? You mean you have to go back and get re-analysed? That's crazy!' Beck claims that her opinion helped crystallise his own thoughts, for after two and a half years of analysis, he hadn't noticed any changes.
>
> (Weishaar, 1993, p. 19)

The concepts of 'long-term' and 'short-term' therapy are hard to define. A consensus has developed, however, whereby 'short-term' therapy can be defined as being 20 or fewer one-hour sessions and 'long-term' as being therapy of a duration of one year or more (approximately 40 or more such sessions) (Ivey et al., 1997). The expression 'medium-term' is sometimes used to describe 21–39 sessions.

In recent decades, psychological therapy has gradually moved into the mainstream health systems of Britain and the USA. Governmental and insurance-based welfare funding has been subject to constant review (Cummings & Sayama, 1995), so that the therapies have contended with a 'socio-economic climate that values shorter treatments and demonstrated efficacy' (Weishaar, 1993, p. 141).

Outcome research has tended to show that, for most clients, change begins early in therapy and is enhanced by long-term interventions only in some cases (Cummings & Sayama, 1995; Ivey et al., 1997). Sheldon (1995) describes the 'decreasing marginal utility' of therapy over time (p. 16). The short-term nature of Beck's cognitive therapy is first described in Beck et al. (1979b) where the 'typical course of therapy' is defined as 20 sessions over 15 weeks: the client may have two sessions per week during the initial phases, dropping to one per week after 3–4 weeks.

The rationale for short-term cognitive therapy is an empirical one, based on research studies on implementing its structure (Rush & Watkins, 1977) in which the average number of sessions turned out to be 15. Nonetheless, this pattern seems to have set the norm for the length of standard CBT. Most subsequent definitions of typical length are in the 12–20 sessions range.

A more elaborated discussion of the short-term nature of cognitive therapy is given by Beck and Emery (1985). The necessity to fit the number of sessions to individual problems and patterns is acknowledged: some specific anxieties may be treated in fewer sessions, and individual patients may require extra time. The spirit of this aspect of cognitive therapy, however, is indicated in statements that 'Long-term therapy for anxiety is unnecessary and is, in many cases, undesirable' (p. 171), and 'the pace of therapy is relatively brisk' (p. 171). This short-term emphasis contains a meta-message that problems can be solved.

It is suggested that the therapist 'rushes slowly' (p. 171), and this implies covering important areas but being able to 'move on quickly' (p. 171). Such important areas might be background history and the exploration of original causes, which tends to be kept minimal. As these areas are strongly emphasised in psychodynamic therapy, psychodynamic therapists are often critical of this aspect of cognitive therapy (Persons et al., 1996). Beck and Emery (1985, p. 172) offer supplementary guidelines for keeping cognitive therapy time-limited:

1   Keep treatment simple, specific and concrete.
2   Stress homework and ongoing assessments.

3 Stay task-relevant and use time management.
4 Develop a brief-intervention mindset and stay focused on manageable problems.

The business-like spirit is less emphasised in the parallel set of principles given by Judith Beck (1995, p. 7):

> Cognitive therapy aims to be time limited . . . [but] not all patients make enough progress in a few months. Some patients require 1 or 2 years of therapy to modify very rigid dysfunctional beliefs & patterns of behaviour.

We see a shift whereby time limits change from a given to an aim, perhaps because of the advent of the 'schema-focused therapy' model (Young et al., 2003) and dialectical behaviour therapy (Linehan, 1993). Young et al. (2003) describe how the evolution of schema-focused therapy began, as they found that some of the assumptions underlying the 'standard model' of cognitive therapy – for example, that clients have good access to thoughts, and could make a therapeutic relationship relatively easily – did not fit a significant minority of patients with more difficult problems.

When these assumptions are not met, therapy is likely to go beyond the 20-session limit. Some critics have considered that there has been a 'psychoanalytic drift' (Milton, 2001) – likely to threaten the parsimony of the initial model – inherent cognitive therapy.

There has been comparatively little research into the effects of different lengths of psychological therapy (Roth & Fonagy, 2005). This is perhaps surprising given the socio-economic imperative towards briefer work. A large cost-benefit analysis was conducted as part of the Kaiser Permanente studies, run over 25 years between the 1960s and the 1980s (Cummings & Sayama, 1995). The results showed that, for around 85 per cent of clients, many of the measurable benefits of therapy were achieved in the first 10 sessions, and 'diminishing returns' were evident thereafter. This might be taken as a straightforward rationale for brief therapy, but around 10 per cent of clients need more than 20 sessions and the other 5 per cent may need much longer-term therapy.

Beck has stressed the need for appropriate 'pacing' of therapy, and this requires 'sufficient control', tempered by sensitivity to individual client needs, to optimise appropriate use of time (Young & Beck, 1980, p. 8).

Beck has made an influential contribution to the development of short-term therapy by showing how effective it can be. This allows treatment to percolate down to more of the patient population. Most therapists, however, even those who prefer short-term work, agree that some clients require longer periods of therapy. The real differences between models may depend on how large this group is estimated to be (Cummings & Sayama, 1995). Beck has been careful to combine advocacy of short-term therapy with the desirability of longer-term work with some clients.

21

Cognitive therapy is structured and directional

> The cognitive therapist is more active and exercises more initiative than does the therapist conducting traditional psychotherapy. . . . He titrates his degree of activity according to the patient's apparent need for structure. . . . The degree of activity and structuring requires an exquisite sensitivity to the client's needs and reactions. No other aspect of cognitive therapy entails as many risks or requires as much skill.
>
> (Beck et al., 1979b, pp. 65–66)

The debate about structure is sometimes confused because the term 'structure' is used in two rather different but interrelated ways. Firstly, structure may refer to a series of behavioural steps that the therapist and/or client can follow within a session or series of sessions. Cognitive therapy has a definite session structure to be followed quite closely (Beck, 1995). The structure consists of a number of sequential steps, beginning with conducting a 'mood check' on how the client is feeling and then setting an agenda for the session. Agenda items, including checking homework tasks, are then pursued as session targets. The session finishes by setting a new homework task and by taking client feedback on the session. Structure in this sense can also be extended to the characteristic shape of the therapeutic intervention over time; for example, CBT usually begins by targeting symptom relief and proceeds later to preventative work on underlying vulnerabilities (Beck et al., 1979b; Wells, 1997).

One rationale for structure of this kind is that clients are often in a confused and chaotic period of their life and are emotionally aroused during counselling. Therapy structure can offer helpful boundaries within which this confusion and arousal can be contained. Therapists may sometimes forget that therapy is an unfamiliar experience for many clients. When clients know the structure it may be easier for them to learn their role in the therapy. Alford and Beck (1997) also argue that structure enhances the collaborative transfer of learning from the therapy context to the real-life context.

Structured sessions are directional in that they are structured to the end of goal attainment. Sheldon (1995) notes that structured approaches within social and therapeutic work are associated with greater effectiveness. Both structure and direction need, however, to be negotiated with the client. Two aspects of the structure are especially helpful in conducting such negotiation: agenda-setting (collaborative agreement of issues to be tackled in the therapy session) and taking feedback (evaluating the client's perception of the usefulness of the session). Some clients are undoubtedly resistant to structure or direction, or to both (Beutler et al., 1994). Responsiveness to client reactions to structure is part of the interpersonal dimension of cognitive therapy – see Point 17. While it is recommended that the cognitive components of this resistance be explored (Leahy, 2003), it is often also helpful to adjust structure and/or direction.

A second usage of the term 'structure' in therapy may refer to the 'deep structure' of the therapy (Ivey et al., 1997). This kind of structure lies in the therapist's ways of understanding the client's problems and assumptions about the underlying psychological change processes in therapy. Another collaborative value of cognitive therapy, however, is to try to make this structural rationale as explicit as possible to the client:

Structure is necessary for collaboration. Patients must learn how improvement is obtained in order to view themselves as collaborative partners in the therapeutic enterprise. To teach patients in this manner, therapists must themselves possess a theoretical rationale for specific treatment techniques.

> Otherwise, there is no structure on which to base the process of collaboration. . . . The American Board of Professional Psychology states explicitly that to earn the ABPP Diploma, a psychologist must treat or make recommendations 'in a meaningful and consistent manner . . . backed by a coherent rationale'.
>
> (Alford & Beck, 1997, p. 12)

'Direction' is perhaps another term that can be easily confused; in this case, with the Rogerian terms, 'directive' and 'non-directive'. It has been argued that CBT is directive and thus works against client self-determination. By using the terms 'offering direction' and 'being directional', one can clarify that 'accepting direction' and 'maintaining self-determination' are not mutually exclusive concepts (Hudson & Macdonald, 1986). It may also be helpful to consider the opposite of 'directional', which is 'directionless' (Bandura, 1969, quoted in Sheldon, 1995, p. 25).

In practice, therapists have to strike a 'balance between being directive and imposing structure on the one hand, and allowing the patient to make choices and take responsibility on the other. This balance involves deciding when to talk and when to listen; when to confront and when to back off; when to offer suggestions and when to wait for the patient to make his/her own suggestions (Young & Beck, 1980, p. 8).

In his various demonstrations of therapy, in live or recorded sessions, Beck shows that it is possible to wear the structure lightly. He also implies that the prime structure is in the therapist's internal template of where therapy is moving, rather than a series of rigid behavioural steps. This author believes that while in general a structured approach offers clients the best deal, it is sometimes important for the therapist to respond strongly to the client's individual needs, which may be for structure but also for toning down structure.

Feedback is also very important. The above points about the style of therapy allude to the necessity of fitting the therapy to the client. It is impossible to do this without having regular feedback based on open and honest discussion with the client. Feedback mechanisms are built into the therapy itself in terms of individual session ('How did this session go?') and periodic reviews ('How are we doing after six sessions?'). Beck himself seems driven by an incredible curiosity about what other people think. I once had the unnerving experience, after one of his demonstrations in Oxford, of finding myself in the next stall of the urinal to him. He asked me what I had thought about his session. I wanted to say – but did not then dare – 'Look, Tim, I know you're really into feedback but there's a time and a place for everything!'

22

Cognitive therapy is problem- and goal-oriented

All therapy models must have goals, but the behavioural tradition has always held that such goals should be *overt* (Hudson & Macdonald, 1986). Problem solving in cognitive therapy is one of the inheritances from the behavioural model (Beck, 1970b). The emphasis on problem solving can clearly be seen in the comments by Beck and Emery (1985) on how to keep therapy manageable referred to earlier. They stress working on manageable problems and offer an important rationale for brevity:

> Because cognitive therapy is time-limited, many of the patient's problems will remain unsolved at the end of treatment. By the time treatment ends, the patient will have enough psychological tools to approach and solve problems on his own, knowing that the therapist is available for booster sessions if necessary.
>
> (Beck & Emery, 1985, p. 172)

The transfer of skills implied above encourages the client to develop the potential to become her own therapist. Brewin (1996) explores the evidence regarding the effective elements of CBT treatment and concludes that the transfer of problem-solving skills is likely to be one of the most effective elements. There is evidence that one of the main advantages of cognitive therapy for depression is that it promotes relapse prevention by increasing the client's ability to solve problems after therapy (Hollon et al., 1996). Jacobson and Hollon (1999a, 1999b) also show that much of the efficacy of cognitive therapy with depression may well lie in relatively simple problem-solving skills that can be taught by non-therapist staff. These findings are reflected in more recent recommendations for the development of 'low-intensity interventions' in the treatment of depression (Roth & Pilling, 2007).

Beck and Emery (1985, p. 171) invoke a deliberately business-like and problem-solving spirit by arguing that specifying a certain number of sessions 'puts in a task-orientated frame for *getting down to business*'. Although almost all therapies probably do aim to solve problems, they may not have such a clear focus on 'problem solving' as that presented in cognitive therapy. The focus on problem solving is closely related to a preference for the briefer time frame. As both psychodynamic and humanistic therapy, especially in traditional form, do not have this short-term emphasis, so they also seem to have characteristically different ways of solving problems, often focusing 'on underlying mechanisms' rather than overt problems.

Various cognitive and behavioural approaches to problem solving have stressed concrete and specific steps in the process (D'Zurilla & Nezu, 1999). These concrete steps invariably focus more on managing overt problems better, rather than the more psychodynamic focus on modifying the 'underlying mechanisms' or the supposed origins of the problem. Such problem solving is particularly helpful when it takes the client's current problem-solving style into account (Sheldon, 1995). Humanistic therapists such as Rogers have favoured exploring around problems, perhaps looking at the possibility of coming at them sideways. Gestalt therapy has been distrustful of 'rational' approaches to problems. Its founder, Fritz Perls, suggested that humans should 'lose their minds and come to their senses' (Clarkson & Mackewn, 1993).

Some recent approaches to CBT have, however, suggested that CBT practitioners may indeed have been over-rational in their approach to problem solving (Hayes et al., 2004). Hayes et al. (2004), for example, suggest that it is important to consider what strategies the client has used previously to solve the problem. Sometimes the client may be trying to use the therapy to buttress a dysfunctional solution: e.g., to 'prove' to a partner that her 'nagging' is causing the client to abuse alcohol. Hayes et al. (2004) therefore suggest that it is important to invest more effort in ensuring that the client has 'accepted' their problem and is 'committed' to changing it. Problem solving that preceded such efforts could easily prove premature and ultimately unsatisfactory. This line of reasoning, however, is not advocating abandoning rational problem solving per se but is suggesting that change processes themselves may have non-rational elements.

The relatively short-term nature of cognitive therapy may also have meant that it has tended to focus on more sharply defined problems in order to make best use of its more limited time perspective. Cognitive therapy has followed the behavioural tradition in seeking to define problems in concrete, often behavioural and/or symptoms-based terms. The focus on problems is shown in the development of the concept of the 'problem list' (Fennell, 1989; Persons, 1989), which is a menu of problems discussed and agreed with the client as being the key target areas for change during the therapy. The list is consulted from time to time and at review to ensure that the therapy has tackled the areas that the client came for help with. The problem list can be used as an ongoing guideline about when therapy may be finished and thereby as an aid to maintaining a focus on short-term therapy.

Young and Beck (1980) suggest that cognitive therapy uses a variety of behavioural 'and action-oriented' techniques to help clients cope better with situations. Whereas the behavioural emphasis is on how to cope, the cognitive emphasis in behavioural techniques focuses more on how behaviours are interpreted. While Young and Beck (1980) rightly insist that behavioural tasks should be chosen according to the client's formulation and should also serve as experiments to test beliefs, he and other cognitive therapy writers have not endorsed so clearly the point that purely *behavioural* benefits may *also* accrue from such experiments. They have, however, advocated the view that behavioural methods are the indicated techniques of choice in the early stages of the cognitive therapy of depression (Young & Beck, 1980, p. 19).

23

Cognitive therapy initially emphasises the present time focus

> Since data collection and use of data in cognitive therapy do not require much data, this approach allows for brief psychotherapy. Hence it is economical. In many cases, short term cognitive therapy may take only 10 to 20 sessions.
>
> (Beck, 1976, p. 317)

This principle is one that does seem to distinguish different schools, especially between cognitive/cognitive behavioural therapy and psychodynamic therapy. Beck (1976), however, stresses that there are many commonalities between cognitive therapy and psychoanalysis: mainly their common interest in insight and restructuring aspects of the overall mental organisation of the client. His main differences with psychoanalysis followed from his research into psychoanalytic concepts of depression. His crucial understanding came from the realisation that the psychoanalytic concept of 'introverted hostility' added little to the cognitive concept; indeed, it was superfluous. The Freudian view of emotion was 'convoluted' and 'so far removed from information obtained from patients that it is difficult to test' (Beck, 1976, p. 114). Furthermore, psychoanalytic approaches 'postulate an indirect connection between the source of fear (in anxiety) and the specific content of the fear that the patient experiences' (Beck, 1976, p. 166). This means that the targets for the therapy of anxiety will be indirect and not as efficient as they should be – thus, the rationale for the supposed 'economical' nature of cognitive therapy. Part of this efficiency comes from the fact that 'it is not necessary to get at ultimate causes of his (viz, the client's) misinterpretation of reality – either in terms of their historical antecedents or present "unconscious" roots' (Beck, 1976, p. 319).

In general, cognitive therapy problem formulations have focused on mechanisms maintaining current symptoms. This does not, however, rule out the possibility that there are underlying factors linked to the maintenance system. Salkovskis et al. (1998), for example, postulate a therapy of OCD based on disrupting the maintenance cycle but also acknowledge that there do seem to be certain recurrent early experiences that are evident in clients' backgrounds – where overprotection and overly stressed responsibility form part of childhood experience. Sanders and Wills (2003) also point out that though the maintenance cycle is stressed in the cognitive therapy of panic disorder, it is frequently fruitful to deal also with other development issues; clients, for example, seem to be more vulnerable to panic when both starting and ending relationships.

There is debate about differences in emphasis between focusing on symptoms and focusing on 'underlying' issues. Persons (1989) clearly sees the underlying issues in terms of the mechanisms that result from early experience and shape beliefs and assumptions. Interestingly, in a later paper, Persons et al. (1996) suggest that this kind of model can help psychodynamically oriented practitioners to be more open to CBT.

Judith Beck (1995, p. 7) follows her father's previous guidelines on starting therapy 'with an examination of here and now problems, regardless of diagnosis'. She suggests, however, that there are three circumstances in which the therapeutic focus might switch to the past:

1 when the client strongly indicates a wish to explore past issues
2 when current problem-focused work falters
3 when the therapist judges that it is particularly important to understand the origin of the ideas.

The last point in particular seems to imply that there is a range of balances between present- and past-focused work that could be regarded as cognitive therapy. Therapists are bound to have slightly different ideas on such a balance – even when they are working with the same approach. The 'uniformity myth' (Kiesler, 1966) argument has, for example, highlighted that differences within schools may be just as significant as differences between schools.

Given that Beck started life as a convinced dynamic therapist, it is fascinating to observe the way that past experience has kept coming back into cognitive therapy in different ways – perhaps ironically, it does seem like the 'presenting past' (Jacobs, 2006). It is still true, however, that most cognitive therapists deal with past experience in a different way from therapists working with other models. From a skill perspective, I believe that Beck gives a masterclass in digging out the client's core beliefs in the well-known 'Richard' tape (Psychological and Educational Films, 1986). After listening to Richard's account of his childhood, Beck asks him, 'What kind of beliefs do you think came out of that childhood?' Not all clients can go directly to thinking about how they were affected by childhood, but as a parsimonious template question, it is not a bad place to start.

24

Cognitive therapy uses an educational model

> It is helpful for the therapist to view himself as a teacher of anxiety-management skills.
>
> (Beck & Emery, 1985, p. 185)

The rationale for an educational approach to therapy comes from the fact that learning has always taken a central role in the behavioural and cognitive approaches in both general psychology and psychotherapy. Cognitive therapists often use the term 'psycho-education' (Hawton et al., 1989) to describe this aspect of their practice. This term seems to be used in two slightly different ways. In the first use of the term, the therapist seeks to help the client to 'learn to learn' (Beck, 1976, p. 229): that is, to learn how to open one's thinking and behaviour to other possibilities. This is important in therapeutic work because clients may be stuck in the so-called neurotic paradox: they may fail to learn from negative experiences and keep repeating the same mistakes.

The second sense in which 'psycho-education' is used is that of offering the client new information from a psychologically informed point of view. It seems likely that more clients are now accessing information about their psychological problem areas and possible treatments from the Internet. The quality of Internet information may, however, be highly variable. Some clients are therefore still likely not to be well informed about the nature of depression, for example, and may regard some of the symptoms as being more pathological than they actually are. Furthermore, if they are depressed, their thinking about their own condition is likely to be influenced by the pessimism and negative attention bias that we know are characteristic of depressive thinking (Beck, 1967).

Even when appropriate psycho-educational information is available, it cannot be safely assumed that clients will easily assimilate it. There is good evidence that patients in general medical settings do not assimilate key health information (Williams et al., 2000), and this may be even more pronounced in the field of psychological therapy. It is because of this problem of the assimilation of more functional information that psycho-education is tackled in a systematic way by cognitive therapists.

Psycho-education is also evident in other therapeutic models – though some humanistic practitioners have expressed reservations about psycho-education, probably because of the assumption of 'expert knowledge' that lies at its heart.

Debates about 'patient empowerment' in health services often focus on the nature of treatment programmes and individuals' responses to them. Cahill (1996) conducts a review of the literature on patient participation and gives the following criteria to assess genuine participation:

1 There should be a relationship between the treatment agent and the patient.
2 The knowledge gap between the two should be narrowed.
3 The treatment agent's power should be surrendered to a degree.
4 The process should result in selective activities.
5 The patient should make a positive gain from the process.

Treatment protocols have played an important role in the development of cognitive therapy. Most protocols contain a psycho-educational phase (Beck et al., 1979b). The five criteria above are generally well covered in the cognitive therapy literature – for example, the emphasis on collaboration, feedback and the therapeutic relationship.

The issue of power is obviously a complex one. CBT has been criticised for not addressing the issue of social power and of not adopting a 'power-sensitive' perspective (Spong & Hollanders, 2003). Critics, however, do not always follow Weber's useful distinction between power and authority – Weber defines authority as legitimate power (Gerth & Wright Mills, 1991). Clients give therapists at least some legitimacy by voluntarily entering into a relationship with them. Beyond that point, abuse of legitimacy or power is somewhat protected by professional codes of ethics. If cognitive therapists follow the suggested structure and protocols, they may minimise potential abuse by explaining the rationale for interventions, seeking feedback from clients, and trying to keep therapy as parsimonious as possible. Young and Beck (1980, p. 7) point out, however, that

Although the patient and therapist share responsibility for the therapy, the effective therapist must be able to use the leverage accorded to him as the professional when necessary.

Humanistic reservations about therapist 'expertise' may not have considered distinguishing between 'being an expert' and 'having expertise'. A client may frequently expect that the therapist will lay claim to some expertise. The therapist can, however, regard her expertise as expertise about people in general but believe that this will be of little avail unless it can ally itself with the client's expertise about her own life (Sanders & Wills, 2005). This view is consonant with the concept of 'collaborative empiricism' described by Beck et al. (1979b).

Humanistic therapy has been especially influenced by the 'anti-psychiatry' movement of the 1960s and 1970s, and this position has been revived again recently within humanistic therapy:

It is not just that psycho-diagnosis is wrong – it is that it is part of a system of evil. (Sanders, 2004, quoting John Shlien)

There is an interesting historical twist here in that there is a case to be made for the early British behavioural therapists, such as Meyer and others, who developed the 'Middlesex approach', as more effective opponents of the 'medical model' in psychiatry than the 'anti-psychiatry' movement. The behavioural therapists set up effective alternative treatments based on idiographic formulation of the patients in opposition to 'symptom-based treatment' (Bruch & Bond, 1998). Paradoxically, cognitive therapists in more recent times have been more content to work within symptom-based protocols, though they would also favour combining such work with an idiographic formulation of the client (Beck, 1995).[1] As some of the 'expertise' claimed by cognitive therapists would involve, for example, the pragmatic use of DSM terminology, person-centred therapists with an 'anti-psychiatry' perspective might well find this aspect of cognitive therapy hard to accept. Many cognitive therapists are located within psychiatric settings (British Association for Behavioural and Cognitive Psychotherapies (BABCP), 2005: personal communication) and may therefore seem to be 'guilty by association' with psychiatry.

Beck's contribution has added a particular cognitive flavour to psycho-education in both the many types of leaflets, such as on how to understand how depression might affect the client, through to the emphasis on checking the client's understanding of what is going on in therapy via 'capsule summaries' (Young & Beck, 1980, p. 5). Far from being an arm of 'oppressive psychiatry', this is part of a major attempt to make psychiatric services both more effective and more humane.

Note

1 There is further discussion of this point under consideration in Points 1, 16 and 17.

25

Homework is a central feature of cognitive therapy

The educational, or psycho-educational, emphasis of cognitive therapy is also evident in the advocacy of 'homework'. This term essentially refers to the tasks that clients may be asked to undertake between therapy sessions. Homework assignments can operate over different areas of behaviour and cognition and these levels may be stressed in different phases of therapy. Early homework assignments can include reading some specific information about, for example, depression or a specific anxiety problem.

Later on, homework may become more experiential – for example, a client who has difficulties relating to others because of social anxiety may be asked to open a low-risk conversation and, at the same time, be aware of his negative thoughts and feelings – a 'behavioural experiment' (Bennett-Levy et al., 2004) designed to test the negative thought that 'Other people are not interested in what I have to say.'

Several innovative aspects of homework are becoming evident in cognitive therapy, including the use of video recording, email and the Internet. There have been several trials using CD-ROM-based CBT materials – often now part of a 'stepped care' approach (Williams, 2002) that attempts to stimulate wider dissemination of CBT by interventions that vary the amount of information materials and therapist time on a sliding scale. CBT therapists may need to be careful that they do not hand a weapon to management for limiting services by participating in these schemes.

The rationale for the homework principle in cognitive therapy theory begins from the assumption that psychological change is difficult and unlikely to come from the generation of insights alone (Beck, 1988). Homework tasks may focus on different levels of change. Listening to a session tape is a deliberately low-key activity and aims to ensure that this, usually early, task is one that the client can do, thus reinforcing therapy as a 'self-efficacious' experience. Some tasks, such as keeping thought records, are intended to reinforce skills learnt in sessions as well as being valuable interventions in themselves. Behavioural experiments are seen as particularly powerful homework tasks, aiming to act as immediate experiential disconfirmation of negative beliefs.

These activities emphasise two strategic factors: that cognitive therapy has taken an intentionally systematic approach to ensure generalisation, and that gains in therapy transfer to the client's everyday life (Ivey et al., 1997). Hollon et al. (1996) have hypothesised that this dimension of CBT explains why it shows greater gains in current methods for measuring efficacy and effectiveness than some other approaches: mostly by helping to guard against relapse during follow-up.

Authors reviewing the use of homework tasks in psychotherapy have been concerned to find out what factors influence compliance with and resistance to the completion of homework tasks, and whether it has been possible to estimate the degree to which homework completion influenced therapy outcomes.

Levels of resistance to homework tasks can be quite high, and practitioners often report difficulties with setting homework (March, 1997). The standard advice for cognitive therapists has been to set the homework tasks as 'no lose' experiments and to start them in session before setting them as homework:

It is helpful when setting up assignments initially to stress that useful data can be obtained even if the patient does fail to do her homework. In this way, the patient who does not do the homework is less likely to brand herself a failure.

(Beck, 1995, p. 255)

If clients do not experience homework as meaningful, it may well lead to dropout. Leahy (2001) argues that non-compliance with homework can often be related to the clients' 'self-limiting strategies', designed to avoid further loss, humiliation or regret. Leahy (2001) suggests that therapists can help by identifying such strategies, examining the negative implications of achieving goals, and encouraging clients to accept their own limitations.

Studies have tended to show that when clients do complete homework assignments, they are much more likely to make and to maintain gains in therapy. There may, however, be other mediating variables that affect outcomes – for example, the types of clients who are prepared to do homework tasks might in any case be more likely to make gains regardless of any therapeutic activity that they had undertaken (Kazantzis et al., 2005a).

Kazantzis (2000) and Kazantzis et al.'s (2000) meta-analyses of studies researching the effect of homework in psychotherapy show an increasing number of studies with quite large sample sizes showing positive results; many of the studies, however, generated only small power levels, so that effect sizes themselves were very variable.

Kazantzis et al. (2005b) show that CBT therapists report a significantly greater use of homework tasks than practitioners of other modalities, though the differences of usage rates among different orientations were not great.

Therapists have sometimes reported a sense of inhibition about asking clients to do homework, and this may relate to a 'person-centred' belief that to do so would put them in an 'expert' or 'teacher' role and thus threaten the therapeutic relationship by appearing patronising (Mooney & Padesky, 1998; Persons, 1989). Humanistic and psychodynamic therapies, however, put more emphasis on the role of insight in generating psychological change and do not have the same imperative that CBT does to get the client to be active and to experiment with her behaviour. Some other therapists may regard setting CBT homework as 'pushy'. Interestingly,

Kazantzis et al. (2005b) report this attitude to homework even among trainees on a CBT diploma course in New Zealand.

Reluctance to use homework may also be related to the strong emphasis that other therapies place on the therapeutic relationship and the therapeutic encounter. Stricker (2006, p. 221), for example, reviews the use of homework in psycho-dynamic therapy and notes that

> To assign homework would seem to deviate from the framework because it places the therapist in the role of an active, directive authority. . . .

> [However] there are few practitioners of psychodynamic psychotherapy who do not ask their patients to remember their dreams, perhaps even to write them down. . . . This is a type of journaling that would be recognizable to any prac-titioner of cognitive behaviour therapy, although that is hardly the specific assignment that would be given.

Although the use of homework would be incompatible with 'the strict application of . . . psychoanalysis' (p. 236), it is possible to devise a set of criteria for its use in 'an assimilative, integrative model of psychodynamic therapy' (p. 219), in which homework would be highly individualised and non-prescriptive.

To summarise, psycho-educational and homework tasks have played a key role in the development of cognitive therapy, especially in attempts to maximise the chances that gains made in therapy are generalised to both life outside sessions and life after therapy finishes. There is evidence that homework does enhance therapy outcomes, though there may be other medi-ating variables. Homework tasks have been used in other active modes of therapy but have perhaps been inhibited in some schools of therapy by a very strong emphasis on the inter-personal and experiential encounter in the therapy session itself. Even in those modes of therapy, however, there is also evidence of an increasing willingness to consider homework tasks as additional options in therapy. Kazantzis and Ronan (2006) have suggested that the use of homework is a candidate for consideration as a 'common factor' in modern psychotherapy.

Beck's contributions have greatly aided the development of the homework concept and they can be seen as crucial in strengthening outcomes in therapy – a point that is increasingly being utilised in most types of therapy. Health authorities are increasingly supplying 'book prescription' schemes as homework backup to other elements of treatment (Frude, 2005).

The following Points now focus on more explicit use of techniques based on the idea that gradual development of awareness of negativity promotes change. Both Aaron (1976) and Judith Beck (1995) distinguish between the processes of *identifying* negative cognitions and *modifying* them. Further they also distinguish a phase for *evaluation* of negative thoughts and beliefs and this phase acts as a transition between identification and change. They both also use the word 'elicitation' – 'drawing forth, evoking a response from a person' (Stevenson, 2007, *Shorter Oxford English Dictionary*) – to emphasise the therapist's role in stimulating these responses.

The fact that there are two stages prior to modification underlines the dangers of being overeager to promote cognitive change and thereby risk enhancing resistance: cognitive therapists should not, after all, act 'like high pressure salesmen' (Young & Beck, 1980, p. 20). Judith (Beck, 1995) offers particularly helpful guidelines to avoid such an approach.

The first step towards change is 'decentring' from the negative thoughts following Socratic dialogue. Classical Socratic dialogue, however, often results in 'aporia':

Socrates describes the purgative effect of reducing someone to aporia: it shows someone who merely thought he knew something that he does not in fact know it and instills in him a desire to investigate it.

(http://enwikipedia.org/wiki/Aporia, accessed 10 April 2008)

Festinger (1957) decribes cognitive dissonance in similar terms, a gap in knowledge that motivates the person to think more deeply about the problem. Sometimes *identifying* and becoming aware of a problem is enough to begin the change process – 'Do I *really* think that?' Once the person has begun to doubt the original idea, he will often naturally move into *evaluating* it. If the evaluation of the idea suggests that it is invalid or not useful, then the person is likely to *modify* or change it.

Points 26–27, following, will deal with identifying, evaluating and modifying cognitions and cognitive processes that are unhelpful to clients. The Points will particularly focus on negative automatic thoughts but will also note how cognitive therapy techniques will vary when dealing with beliefs and assumptions. The points will use the structure of the seven-column thought record (Greenberger & Padesky, 1995) to illustrate the processes of identification (columns 1–3), evaluation (columns 4–5) and modification (columns 6–7). The keynote methods for working with negative thoughts are Socratic questioning and dialogue and guided discovery. Point 28 will describe the processes used to identify, evaluate and modify cognitive processes.

26

Cognitive therapists teach clients to evaluate and modify their thoughts

As was shown in Part 1, the problematic elements of negative thoughts are evident in their forms (distorted), their content (psycho-pathogenic) and their meaning (unhelpful), and it is at these elements that the Socratic processes are aimed.

The process often begins from a client's 'mood report' recorded as part of a homework task or as a mood shift observed during a session. The therapist needs to explain the rationale of working with negative thoughts, and this is often achieved by the explanation that negative thoughts seem to result in negative emotions – so it seems feasible that changing such thoughts may lead to a change in mood for the better. This is a pragmatic and empirical assertion – made on a 'let us see what happens' basis. The client's ability to identify and link thoughts and feelings may be tested via 'thought-feeling' exercises (Wills, 2008).

Hollon and Kendall (1980) have devised a questionnaire to identify negative thoughts, but many therapists prefer to find the negative thoughts that are embedded in the client's context and daily reality. It is helpful to get clients to identify the specific moment when the NATs 'kick in'. For example, the general trigger may be the break-up of a relationship, but the negative thoughts might become much clearer when a client thinks, for example, about the fact that he has no one to go out with for a meal on his birthday. A specific situation is more likely to reveal thoughts linked to strong negative emotions, and this effect can be accentuated by getting the client to describe the event as if it were happening now – in first person, present tense form (Simmons & Wills, 2006). The therapist uses guided discovery and Socratic questions to dig under the surface for the negative meaning embedded in these experiences. Clients are often helped to 'see' and 'hear' what they have been thinking by writing the thoughts on a whiteboard. Many clients have told me that they can visualise their thoughts on a whiteboard and that this has helped them to respond to such thoughts better. It is vital to reach the emotional salience of the events, and if the events have a strong interpersonal dimension, this can be further enhanced by a role play in which the therapist plays the other person involved (Beck, 1995).

In Figure 5, identifying negative thoughts is represented by the first three columns of the seven-column thought record, identifying trigger, emotion and thought (or image) respectively. The three elements can be written into the thought record or up on the whiteboard as a 'vicious cycle' diagram. The therapist should have an eye on the overall formulation during this process, and this should help her to identify thoughts that are likely to be central to the client's most troubling symptoms.

As the thoughts become evident, the client can spot themes running through them – for example, cognitive specificity content (in anxiety thoughts about danger and threat) and particular types of cognitive distortion (in anxiety and catastrophisation). The therapist is looking for 'hot thoughts' (Greenberger & Padesky, 1995) – ideally, clients should be able to appreciate how these thoughts are linked to their problems. The therapist tries to explore and target 'key cognitions' (Young & Beck, 1980) – evaluation of those thoughts often seems to emerge naturally. The more experience the therapist accumulates, the more she is able to see pointers to develop cognitive change work. For example, in social anxiety, research on the typical accompanying thoughts sensitises the therapist to look for signs that the clients may be over-interpreting signals that imply people may be taking a critical stance toward them (Wells, 1997). The client may, for example, say, 'I felt that everyone was looking askance at me.' The therapist is alerted to

Trigger	Emotion	NAT	Evidence for NAT	Evidence against NAT	Alternative adaptive thought	Outcome
Blood on money from cashpoint	Anxious 80 per cent	I have got dangerous germs on my hands. I could kill my son and husband.	Germs are everywhere.	Germs are only very rarely dangerous. Blood infections aren't that hardy.	I may have germs on my hands, but they are almost certainly harmless.	Anxiety 30 per cent Resist washing hands/changing clothes

Figure 5 Seven-column thought record: worked example (adapted from Greenberger & Padesky, 1995)

the possibility of over-interpretation of this material and the possibility of cognitive distortions – overgeneralisation and emotional reasoning (Beck & Emery, 1985). The therapist's radar picks this up and uses clinical judgement to ask a series of questions aimed to open up this area – What were people doing? How many of them pulled faces? Were there any people who you think might have been a bit more sympathetic to you?

Judith Beck (1995) describes things that may go wrong in identifying and evaluating negative thoughts and matches each problem with a helpful antidote. For example, clients may report not being able to identify specific thoughts or feelings; one good countermove is for the therapist to suggest the opposite feeling or thought, and this often results in the vigorous statement of a highly appropriate thought or feeling. Another problem is that actual thoughts may be secreted in questions such as 'I thought to myself, "why me?"' (I'm a loser), or statements such as 'Typical' (I always have bad luck). The therapist must then probe for the hidden thought by asking, 'Why do you think these things happen to you?' (Wills, 2008). Finally, clients may have very real life problems, so that their negative thoughts can seem only too realistic. Although they may achieve 'rational insight' into the problem, this insight may not always carry 'emotional conviction'. This point becomes more crucial during the modification phase, when the therapist can both enact the virtues of empathising with the client's difficulties and encourage sheer persistence in using cognitive methods. As Aaron Beck has commented, 'One swallow does not make a summer' (Psychological and Educational Films, 1986).

Beliefs and assumptions often are identified from the themes that persistently run through NATs. Usually, NATs are tackled first in cognitive therapy, so that the client has already been working on the belief level by targeting NATs. The therapist's main task with beliefs and assumptions in the identification and evaluation stage is to make them explicit and testable. 'Rules', for example, can be turned into 'if/then' format statements. 'I can't trust people' can, for example, be converted into 'If I trust people, then they will take advantage.' The assumption in this form more clearly has problematic effects on the person's life – it is also more testable. Beliefs and assumptions should also be tested against the overall formulation – if thoughts, assumptions and beliefs seem to operate together, then the client is more able to see how they limit him, and, conversely, the need to modify them becomes more apparent. Because beliefs tend to be both enduring and inflexible, additional factors, such as behavioural experiments and imagery work, may be added to the strategies list for tackling them.

Beck provided systematic procedures for identifying negative thoughts in his early publications. The extensive array of methods has been significantly expanded by many subsequent cognitive therapists, including Judith Beck.

27

Cognitive therapy uses various methods to change cognitive content

As evaluation of negative thoughts proceeds, therapist and client gather more and more data to weigh the relative merits of thoughts and beliefs, and turn to this variety of methods to evaluate and change them. Padesky and Greenberger (1995) make the useful procedural suggestion that it is helpful to consider evidence that supports the negative thought under scrutiny first. This counter-intuitive suggestion makes sense when we realise that it is often the overeager salesman who is the least convincing. The cognitive therapist does truly want the client to make up his own mind but also realises that over-presenting a case can induce resistance. This view coincides with Safran and Segal's (1990) idea that cognitive restructuring is often most effective when the client is 'fully immersed' in his negative thoughts. When a client is in 'two minds' about such thinking, therapist interventions may be unhelpfully embroiled in his internal debate. The testing of beliefs is 'inductive' and Socratic because it proceeds from the theory inherent in the client's thought and then tests that thought against available evidence.

Judith Beck (1995, p. 125) states that the purpose of the thought modification phase is to 'fortify' alternative perspectives emerging from thought evaluation. Aaron Beck (1976, p. 6) stresses the fact that cognitive therapy bears a strong resemblance to the normal processes of 'common sense'. When we face everyday problems, we often have a process of reviewing the facts of the case, deciding the most likely explanation, and then responding to that situation. The structure of a

Common-sense steps	Thought record columns	Client example (simplified)
Identification of problem	1 Event 2 Emotion	1 My boyfriend's 'cool' reaction to my good exam result 2 Hurt, angry (85 per cent)
Identification of meaning	3 Negative thought/s	3 He doesn't love me No one will ever love me
Reflection on initial appraisal of meaning	4 Evidence supporting negative thought	4 He often does things like this My mum didn't love me
Reflection on initial appraisal of meaning	5 Evidence not supporting negative thought	5 He does nice things sometimes He finds it hard to respond to my overwhelming needs at times He's a young man He may be a bit jealous Mum's tried to make up for past wrongs
Reappraisal of initial meaning allocation	6 Alternative, balanced thought	6 We both need to work on how to ask for things and respond to each other
Consideration of consequences of reappraisal	7 Outcome	7 Emotional – feeling much less hurt and angry Behavioural: I can try assertively asking for what I want without being overemotional

Figure 6 Common-sense processes reinforced by a thought record (adapted from Greenberger & Padesky, 1995) with a client example

thought record spells out such a process to help the depressed or anxious person use these common-sense processes that may be currently blocked off from them. This point is reinforced by examining how common-sense steps are reflected in the thought record (Figure 6).

The fact that thought records are written and can be kept and mulled over adds to their capacity to 'fortify' adaptive changes in thinking.

Working with negative thinking often comprises several different cycles of verbal and written work. Initial work may involve verbal recognition of thought-feeling patterns, which are then written onto a whiteboard. Later cycles involve spotting such patterns in other areas and then writing them down into thought records, with the accompanying steps to facilitate adaptive change.

In this version of the thought record (Figures 5 and 6), columns 1, 2 and 3 represent a way of identifying the negative thought and feeling pattern, columns 4 and 5 show a way of evaluating it, and finally, columns 6 and 7 represent a way of fortifying the change process. Column 6 is sometimes titled 'rational response', but I personally prefer Greenberger and Padesky's (1995) usage of 'alternative balanced thought' and find it chimes better with Beck's own avoidance of the word 'irrational' (Weishaar, 1993, p. 119):

Beck eschews the word 'irrational' beliefs in reference to maladaptive thoughts, for at one time in the person's life these beliefs made sense.

It is often helpful to consider the nature and form of the original negative thought when attempting to generate an alternative. For example, if the original contains a clear cognitive distortion, such as 'catastrophisation', then the alternative should naturally seek to de-catastrophise:

Catastrophising thought
This feeling is so bad, it will drive me mad.

Alternative
This feeling is bad but it will pass.
Meanwhile, it is unlikely to drive me mad.

Rebuttals of wrong attributions should seek to reattribute:

I can't decide anything; it means I have 'lost it'.	Decisions are difficult because I feel depressed.

Metaphors can help when generating alternatives:

- What would your 'old self' say about this?
- How might you think about this on a good day?

There are a variety of different thought records; for example, the ABCDE format used in REBT (Ellis & Dryden, 1987) and the 'mood logs' of David Burns (1999). To some extent, therapists can use different elements to construct a thought record that seems to match the client's needs and understanding. Sometimes a particular client may respond well to a particular self-help book, and in this case, it is usually more helpful to use the form of the thought record shown in such a book.

The whole process ends with the client rerating the negative feelings and behaviours described in columns 1–3 and defining how they would now be while holding this new thought in mind (column 7). If the negative feeling is less, even if only by a small amount, then it seems to show that cognitive therapy works – when you change the negative thoughts to something more helpful, the negative emotions and behaviours do seem to be less significant.

There may of course be practical difficulties: the client may fear that the thought record will be read by someone they do not wish to see it. The therapist can use problem solving to explore ways round such difficulties – using a miniature version that can be kept in a shirt pocket.

Beck (1995) and Wills (2008) stress the importance of therapists keeping thought records themselves. This both enhances their ability to win a mandate for keeping thought records from clients and sensitises therapists to the ups and downs of use over a period of time. My own experience taught me that results are quite varied – sometimes they are strong and immediate, at other times, subtle and delayed. I have learnt the virtue of over-practice and persistence in their use – in any case, it is a definite mistake to give up on them too easily. Some writers have recently appeared to argue for the superiority of more experiential techniques such as behavioural experiments for the generation of change (Bennett-Levy, 2003). This seems to me a premature judgement.

Different techniques, such as behavioural experiments, may become more necessary when working on belief change, along with other such techniques as coping cards, imagery, pie charts, continua and role play (Leahy, 2003). This is because beliefs seem to span a wider range of situations, and a stronger battery of techniques may be necessary in these wider contexts. The origin of most of these techniques can be traced to Beck's work.

28

Cognitive therapy uses a variety of methods to change cognitive processes

For Points 26 and 27 in this Part, we have used a largely left-brained vocabulary – speaking of identifying, evaluating and modifying. Turning to the area of change in cognitive processes, we now use a more divergent, right-brained set of words – noticing cognitive processes, watching them and reflecting upon them.

We encountered these terms in Beck and Emery's (1985) AWARE strategy (Part 1, Point 11), in which the client is advised to accept and become aware of anxiety and to watch it without evaluating it. The final step in AWARE is a cognitive content-based instruction to 'expect the best' – combining mindful attentional strategies with cognitive instructions is one of the main themes of this point.

A consensus is now building in cognitive therapy that working with the content of obsessional and ruminative thoughts is usually only partially effective. The problems these thoughts cause are influenced by the attention that clients pay to them. Almost 90 per cent of people have thoughts similar to those that afflict OCD clients (Rachman, 2003). The difference between 'normal' and 'abnormal' obsessions lies in the way that people react to them. Most people can dismiss them without much thought. For OCD sufferers, however, such thoughts are so objectionable and carry such profoundly negative meaning that they attempt to suppress them in a way that only succeeds in producing a 'rebound effect', making the thought ever harder to suppress.

Similarly, the content of worry does not differ much between sufferers and non-sufferers. Worry is functional – up to a point.

People need to be concerned about things that could go wrong in their lives and would be 'unprepared' to meet crises if they were not. Leahy (2005) distinguishes between 'productive worry' and 'unproductive worry'. Butler and Hope (2006) describe how worry is productive when it leads us to take reasonable action in relation to our problems, but is unproductive when 'ruminative worry' blocks such action or prevents us from, as Carnegie puts it, *cooperating with the inevitable*.

It is therefore helpful to develop a different type of relationship to worries, intrusions and obsessions. The way we think about our cognitive processes ('meta-cognition') may determine how far we can overcome these problems, so that rethinking our meta-cognitive beliefs is a helpful first step. Wells (2000) has suggested a number of ways of changing the way we pay attention to negative thoughts, such as rethinking meta-cognitive beliefs and being more 'mindful' about them.

The theoretical understanding of these helpful processes is, however, probably still ahead of more practical versions of how they can be implemented by therapists. Some strands of the new thinking have focused on devising mindfulness programmes to prevent relapse in depression, such as mindfulness-based cognitive therapy (Segal et al., 2002) and attention training (Wells, 2000). Others have focused on how therapists can use some of the methods in one-to-one therapy (Fennell, 2004). Mindfulness is inevitably difficult to put into words and may even involve some deconstruction of language (Hayes et al., 2004).

Leahy's (2005) approach to worry does, however, contain a really useful set of cognitive 'think steps' that can be helpful to clients trying to evolve a less enmeshed relationship with their own tendency to worry. Like Segal et al.'s (2002) mindfulness programme, Leahy's mindfulness steps are woven in with more active cognitive steps focused on restructuring. The seven steps are shown in Figure 7.

The client is encouraged to develop 'mindful detachment', a state that emphasises non-possessive awareness and radical acceptance. Step 2 – accepting reality and committing to

1 Distinguish between productive and unproductive worry.
2 Accept reality and commit to change.
3 Challenge worried thinking.
4 Focus on the deeper threat.
5 Turn failure into opportunity.
6 Use emotions rather than worry about them.
7 Take control of time.

Figure 7 Seven-step worry cure (adapted from Leahy, 2005)

change – clearly owes much to Steve Hayes' ACT model (Hayes et al., 2004). Hayes has been another therapist strongly associated with the 'third wave' in CBT (Sanders & Wills, 2005). It is interesting that the mindful strategies associated with this step 2 come *before* the more traditional cognitive intervention steps, such as challenging thinking in step 3. This implies that it is important for clients to develop a different type of relationship with their worry processes before starting to challenge the content of worrying thoughts. An important function of worry may be to protect the client from feeling certain other negative emotions (Leahy, 2005, p. 293). This disowning of emotion would mean that cognitive work could fail to evoke appropriate emotions and would therefore fail to meet the criteria that would be needed for *metanoia,* a change in heart and mind.

The therapist helps the worried client to become more mindfully engaged in present time because worry is a problem oriented towards the future. Worry can also lead to depression, and depressed thinking is typically global and non-specific. The therapist therefore helps the client to come to and stay in the present moment by describing concrete experience and 'noticing' what is happening around him. Leahy specifies five 'think steps' that the therapist can introduce and then 'walk through' with the client (Figure 8).

To gain distance, we need firstly to remember that a thought is just a thought. A thought is not reality. We can do this by using the formula, 'I am simply having the thought that . . .'

1 Gain distance from your thoughts ('I am simply having the thought that . . .').
2 Describe what is in front of you.
3 Suspend or postpone evaluating or judging your experience.
4 Take yourself out or away from the centre of things.
5 Disappear to see reality: once you are out of it, you can 'see' it.

Figure 8 'Think steps' toward accepting reality by mindfulness (adapted from Leahy, 2005)

and 'I am simply noticing that I am feeling . . .' We can bring our minds into the present moment by looking at what is around us and describing it in simple and concrete terms. At this stage, we can also suspend judgement on our experiences and our thoughts. Evaluation is only ever provisional – the final results are not yet in – as Albert Ellis has reminded us. Evaluation can tie up immense amounts of mental energy, and yet the finding of real value can be elusive. The final moves in Leahy's sequence involve 'taking yourself out of the picture'. This step is taken by imaging the world and life proceeding without you. This may sound scary but can also be very liberating. The effect of all these steps is to take the sting out of nagging and negative effects of worry. A key element is the slowing down and gentling up of thinking processes.

This is indeed new ground for cognitive therapy, one with many attractive possibilities but perhaps some dangers too – I have already known one client who had a major abreaction when exposed to a mindfulness group. Some of Leahy's work reads almost like Zen *kōans* – and perhaps as we get engaged with this type of work, we should be wary of playing the 'guru game':

Change and progress involves successful imperfection and constructive discomfort.

(Leahy, 2005, p. 95)

Beck's contribution has been mainly in the area of his theoretical contributions to the description of attention processes in psychopathology, as described in Part 1. As I have also discussed in Part 2, he has seemed presently to connote the more procedural approaches of Wells (2000) and Leahy (2005) and seems to be waiting for more results on mindfulness-based cognitive therapy with interest. Most interventions in this area combine mindful attention with some more direct cognitive work, and it will be interesting to see how that balance develops over the years.

29

Cognitive therapy uses a variety of methods to promote behavioural change

> For the behaviour therapist, the modification of behaviour is
> an end in itself; for the cognitive therapist it is a means to an
> end – namely cognitive change.
>
> (Beck et al., 1979b, p. 119)

As we saw in Part 1, behaviour has been shown to play a key role in formulation – generally and also in specific contexts such as the role of withdrawal in depression and 'safety behaviour' in anxiety. Cognitive therapists are open to using techniques from behaviour therapy, the main techniques being exposure therapy, graded task assignments, activity scheduling, self-monitoring, behavioural experiments and behavioural diaries (Hersen, 2002). Other behavioural methods, such as contingency management, are described by Sheldon (1995). The only real point of departure between cognitive and behaviour therapy has been the debate about whether these techniques are effective in their own right and/or as reinforcement of cognitive change: in that they disconfirm dysfunctional client cognitions during 'behavioural experiments' (Rachman, 1997a). For example, the client with panic disorder often believes that the panic symptoms will drive her mad. Exposing herself to situations that have triggered panic reactions in the past and refraining from 'safety behaviours' might mean that she can find that she does not go mad. Repeated experiences like this may eventually disconfirm the belief. In the debate between cognitive and behaviour therapists, cognitive therapists have argued that adding cognitive elements to, for example, exposure treatments enhanced their effectiveness whereas behaviour therapists have argued that they made no difference. Each party was able to offer some supportive evidence for its case (Eysenck, 1997; Rachman, 1997b).

The conceptual framework offered by Brewin (1996) has been helpful in resolving this debate. Brewin suggests that one must distinguish, firstly, between 'situationally accessible' and 'verbally accessible' knowledge, and, secondly, between specified and generalised disorders, to understand the relative contributions of cognitive and behavioural interventions in different disorders. Verbally accessible knowledge or insight allows reflective techniques to be effective. Situational knowledge may, however, require a specific type of stimulus to provoke emotionally relevant knowledge. This is often the case in anxiety disorders, where discussion of fear experiences without some feeling of anxiety being actually present does not seem helpful (Foa & Kozak, 1986). Brewin also uses the distinction between specific cognitions linked to specific disorders: for example, the highly specific thinking that goes with panic (Clark, 1996) – and the more generalised cognitions that go with generalised anxiety disorder (Wells, 1997) – to suggest ground rules for choosing the interventions most likely to shift particular types of thinking: sometimes these may be cognitive interventions that shift behaviours and sometimes they will be behavioural interventions that shift cognitions.

I have already commented on the role that Beck gave behavioural therapy techniques in cognitive theory. This step has been matched by carefully thought-out behavioural interventions, based on the formulation, being developed on the practice side. There are many creative adaptations of behavioural interventions, but three main ones, activity scheduling and mastery and pleasure ratings, are used to activate withdrawn and depressed clients. Exposure techniques are used to help anxious clients face and overcome fears. In cognitive therapy, there is always the hope that behavioural interventions work on two levels: firstly, at the level of the behaviour change itself (for example, the depressed client does become more active) and, secondly, at the level of cognitive change (for example, the client's behaviour change leads her to revise her belief that she is incapable of being active again).

Belief change is more explicitly targeted, however, by the use of behavioural experiments (Bennett-Levy et al., 2004). Bennett-Levy et al. (2004) see the emergence of the behavioural experiment concept as one of the most radical developments that has come from Beck's cognitive therapy. They suggest that there are fundamentally two main types of experiment – active ones, in which the client tries doing something differently, and observational ones, in which the client observes situations similar to his own. These observational experiments may be in the form of therapist modelling, surveys or direct observation. After each experiment, the client reconsiders his thoughts and beliefs in light of what he has learnt or observed. Bennett-Levy et al. (2004) offer guidelines for setting up effective experiments. Bennett-Levy (2003) has suggested that behavioural experiments may be more convincing in promoting effective change methods than activities such as keeping thought records because they connect more directly to immediate experiential change. To me, however, this view can be overstated because behavioural experiments to test certain beliefs may be hard to formulate in convincing terms. Some beliefs, such as 'I'll die from the stress I'm under', are long-range predictions and not likely to be disconfirmed over a few afternoons. Additionally, while behavioural experiments may stimulate a more immediate sense of engagement, change usually often also occurs as the result of a more constant 'drip, drip' effect, and thought records may be more effective in that area. Either way, there is no really convincing evidence from client studies, so it may be unwise to over-promote one method at the expense of another at this stage.

Beck's (1970b) landmark paper on the relationship between behaviour therapy and cognitive therapy paved the way for the strong behavioural strand in CBT and may have been key to the integration of the two approaches into CBT (Rachman, 1997a). He gave an early impetus to the behavioural experiment concept and added promising methods to use in the construction of such experiments. These concepts have inspired a wide range of clinicians to expand this tradition.

30

Cognitive therapists have developed the measurement of therapist competence

Beck and his colleagues have worked hard to develop the measurement of competence in cognitive therapy:

> The system of psychotherapeutic techniques is clearly and explicitly defined in our cognitive therapy treatment manuals, especially in the manual for the treatment of depression. The uniformity of treatment procedures has been confirmed by monitoring the interviews (by means of tape recordings) of the psychotherapists in our training research program.
>
> (Beck, 1976, p. 332)

Beck et al. (1979b) used the protocol that had been developed for a large, multi-site depression trial to develop a competency checklist containing 18 different competencies, as shown in Figure 9.

Each competency item specified defined levels of competence. The derivation of these competencies is not discussed, but they were revised into the Cognitive Therapy Scale (CTS) and accompanying manual (Young & Beck, 1980). The competency items were condensed and reduced to 11 items. The CTS scale has been widely used and has shown good reliability and validity (Weishaar, 1993). Some further adjustments were made in 1988 (Young & Beck, 1988). Researchers and trainers at the University of Newcastle undertook a project to improve interrater reliability by offering staff further training in using the scale. This project resulted in a revised scale with 12 items: the Cognitive Therapy Scale Revised (CTS-R) (Milne et al., 2001). Reichelt et al. (2003) reported improved reliability for this revision. These developments represent active attempts to improve competence measurement but give rise to some problems in comparative research, as all three versions are in current use. The different versions of the scale are shown in Figure 9.

The CTS has proved very useful for trainers, not only as a standardised yardstick for measuring competence but also in helping understand the *qualities* that we look for in cognitive therapists. Padesky (1996, pp. 270–271) describes her experience as a trainer and notes that the ability to follow CBT structure must be matched by the ability to form a therapeutic relationship and an understanding of the empirical scientific method.

> Therapists who are not willing to participate in a highly interactive therapeutic relationship are poor candidates for Cognitive Therapy training. . . .The ideal cognitive therapist is capable of being highly structured in therapy, comfortable tracking a number of tasks within a session, and yet sensitive to adapting therapy to individual clients to maximise collaboration and positive therapeutic relationships.

Trainers use the CTS to assess practice tapes submitted by trainees. The use of audio and video recordings was incorporated into the early development of practice and training and has continued since (Beck et al., 1979b; Dryden, 2004; Padesky, 1996). One limiting factor is that courses mainly allow trainees to choose which tapes to submit. This should, however, limit the danger that a trainee might be assessed on the basis of work with an unusually difficult client. The interpretation of CTS ratings varies somewhat from course to course.

A number of studies have compared pre- and post-training measures of CTS scores to establish that trainees *do* make significant gains in skill acquisition during training (Milne et al., 1999; Williams et al., 1991). Two other studies have examined

1979 Checklist (Beck et al., 1979b)	CTS (Young & Beck, 1980)	CTS (Young & Beck, 1988)	CTS-R (Milne et al., 2001)
2) Establishing agenda	1) Agenda setting	1) AGENDA SETTING	**1) Agenda**
3) Elicited reactions to session and therapist	2) Feedback	2) FEEDBACK	**2) Feedback**
	3) Understanding	3) UNDERSTANDING	
18) *Rapport*	4) Interpersonal effectiveness	4) INTERPERSONAL EFFECTIVENESS	**5) Interpersonal effectiveness**
1) Collaboration and mutual understanding	5) Collaboration	5) COLLABORATION	**3) Collaboration**
4) Structured therapy time efficiently	6) Pacing	6) PACING	**4) Pacing**
6) Questioning	7) Guided discovery	7) GUIDED DISCOVERY	**8) Guided discovery**
10) *Elicit NATS* and 11) *Test NATS*	8) Focus on cognition	8) FOCUS ON COGNITION	**7) Focus key cognitions**
		9) CONCEPTUALISATION	**9) Conceptual integration**
5) Focused on appropriate problem	9) Strategy for change	10) STRATEGY FOR CHANGE	
12) *Identify assumptions*	10) Application C and B techniques	11) COGNITIVE TECHNIQUES	**10) Cognitive techniques**

Figure 9 The development of the Cognitive Therapy Scale (CTS)

1979 Checklist (Beck et al., 1979b)	CTS (Young & Beck, 1980)	CTS (Young & Beck, 1988)	CTS-R (Milne et al., 2001)
9) and 13) Appropriate CBT techniques		12) BEHAVIOURAL TECHNIQUES	11) Behavioural techniques
8) Assigned homework	11) Homework	13) HOMEWORK	12) Homework
7) Summaries	Overall assessment	Overall assessment	
14) Genuineness	Specific problems	Specific problems	6) Eliciting emotion
15) Warmth			
16) Accurate empathy			
17) Professional manner			

Figure 9 Continued

the effect of therapist competence measured by the CTS on the outcome of therapy (Shaw et al., 1999; Trepka et al., 2004).

Shaw et al.'s (1999) findings offered 'limited support for the relationship between therapist competence as measured by the CTS (1988 version) and reduction in depressive symptomatology' (Shaw et al., 1999, p. 844). Shaw et al. (1999) noted that there were difficulties in the depression trial that contravened their own previous recommendations, especially for ongoing supervision.

Trepka et al. (2004) also researched the relationship between competence and outcome, but in the context of more routine practice situations. A randomly selected CBT session from each of 30 courses of therapy was rated with the CTS, 1988 version, and another psychotherapy alliance measure. Both therapeutic alliance and therapist competence were related to outcome. In regression analysis, the alliance remained significantly related to outcome when controlling for competence, but not vice versa. These relationships with outcome were primarily attributable to therapist rather than to client attributes. Associations with outcome appeared stronger for clients who completed therapy than for those who did not.

Identifying the different areas of cognitive therapy skills is helpful in that different skills may be associated with different phases of the learning cycle for therapists and with different types of teaching and learning strategies (Bennett-Levy, 2006). Bennett-Levy (2006) suggests that there are differences between knowledge-based skills and clinical judgement. Knowledge skills are learnt in early training, but more advanced training and supervision processes may be needed for the development of reflective and interpersonal skills – especially for the maintenance and repair of therapeutic relationships in difficult situations (Safran & Muran, 2000). Developing such skills requires more self-reflectivity in trainees. Bennett-Levy and Thwaites (2006) suggest that cognitive therapy supervision should be more prepared to take on this function. There is also a debate on whether such training should include personal therapy. Bennett-

Levy and Thwaites (2006) have, however, suggested a process whereby trainees experience therapy with each other as both therapist and client. This can perform the same function as personal therapy and can be monitored more carefully within the training course.

Bennett-Levy and Beedie (2007) have studied how cognitive therapy trainees experience the development of competence during the period of training. Greater difficulty in learning interpersonal skills for cognitive therapy may be accounted for by having to learn manualised procedures. Trainees probably suffer somewhat from divided attention at such times. Similar findings were reported in studies of psychodynamic and interpersonal training studies (Mackay et al., 2001).

All in all, these studies suggest that there is a need for more interpersonal focus in CBT training and that this should be maintained by supervision into post-training. The professional development of therapists after training also draws attention to the need for appropriate environments for ongoing practice.

The establishment of national standards is the first step in developing a wider system of support for therapists because such standards can help agencies with a frame of reference to support the growth of CBT into their areas. Sudak et al. (2003) describe cognitive therapy competency standards for psychiatric resident doctors in the USA. Roth and Pilling (2007) completed a similar set of CBT competencies for the UK, and these seem likely to be used to develop national occupation standards for CBT in the UK.

Beck's formative work on measuring cognitive therapy competencies has meant that, compared to the wider field of psychotherapy, the development of identifying, defining, measuring, teaching and promoting skills in cognitive therapy has been rapid, though there is still much work to be done. The need for responsive training systems has been evident. Such responsiveness is likely to be needed in order to engage trainees who will come for cognitive therapy training having previously absorbed a different therapy model (Wills, 2006, 2008).

Summary and review of Part 2

Aaron Beck has been an unusual figure in the therapy world in that he has combined the roles of a major theoretician and researcher with that of a gifted practitioner. He has stressed the importance of ensuring a strong development of these three elements during the development of cognitive therapy. The only aim of his research and theoretical work was to secure an effective treatment model for clients, and at no time did he take time out of one sphere in order to develop in another. He appears to have juggled the three balls relentlessly throughout. The only period of 'sabbatical' that I have been able to find was when he spent some time in Oxford and wrote his book on couple work (Beck, 1988). This is an interesting point because in talking about this period, Beck said that it allowed him to address some of his critics who had made the point that cognitive therapy did not have much to say about relationships. This effort also nailed another criticism – that cognitive therapy was only interested in emotions defined as symptoms by the *DSM* (Padesky & Beck, 1990). The resulting book is interesting in that it is distinctly less 'clinical' than many of his other publications and perhaps gives an interesting insight into how cognitive therapy might have developed had he not made the, at the time uncertain, decision to work in the psychiatric field (Weishaar, 1993). Additionally, despite being on 'sabbatical', informants at Oxford have told me that he continued to see clients and to give clinical demonstrations. One gets the impression that he does like doing therapeutic work: as people sometimes say of surgeons, 'surgeons *do* like doing surgery', but one feels that Beck would *not* fulfil the unspoken second part of this sentence – 'whether people need surgery or not!'

Beck has been a therapeutic protagonist who has led from the front, like Ellis, Rogers and Freud. Without yet being finished, he has left us many publications and more recorded examples of his practice than any of them – though Ellis must run him a close second. When research did not turn out as Rogers hoped, he turned elsewhere. When Beck's research hit problems, he kept going. Where Freud changed his theories without fully admitting it, Beck has been quick to acknowledge amendments (Beck, 1987, 1988), as has Ellis (Dryden, 1991). While Ellis built a strong base in New York but did not go out of his way to influence clinicians in general, Beck has made both intellectual and practical attempts to influence the practice of all therapists on a global level (Alford & Beck, 1997). Though it has taken most of a lifetime, there are now clear signs that this influence is reaching critical mass (Linklater & Harland, 2006).

Conclusion

I must now turn to the rather daunting task of summarising the achievements of Aaron Beck in a final review. As I have been considering a structure for this section, I have realised that the reason why it is hard is because so much about him and his therapy model hangs together as a whole package that is difficult to disconnect.

The review will begin by considering Beck's theoretical, practical and research achievements and will conclude by viewing these same factors through the lens of him as a person with a fully lived life.

His research and therapy began with their greatest achievement – an effective approach to depression in its various guises and, equally importantly, its most difficult manifestation – suicide. From depression, Beck worked on toward anxiety and then more complex problems such as substance abuse and personality disorders.

He achieved very good results in all these areas because he was concerned first to build up a sound formulation of them and then to road-test interventions focused on the formulation. Unlike much that went before, his formulations were neither 'farfetched' nor 'grossly improbable' (Salkovskis, 1996b, pp. 535 and 538). The shift in perspective from psychoanalysis was 'little' (Linklater & Harland, 2006, p. 39) yet profound. He focused on 'how' rather than 'why' (Weishaar, 1993, p. 133). He realised that the 'motivational' view in psychoanalysis (on 'the need to suffer') was not helpful and that by moving to a simpler view, he was able to dispense with much of the super-structure of analytic theory and practice and to make therapy more parsimonious. This meant that therapy could also take a more collaborative and empowering stance – a 'bold step' (Padesky, 2004, p. 7) given the environment that Beck had operated in and one for which he had to endure a certain amount of isolation and criticism. Therapy was thus 'demys-tified' (Weishaar, 1993, p. 134) though it remained 'a very active and directive form of therapy, which appreciates broader dynamic issues'.

It can be argued that he was here following some of the earlier path of Carl Rogers. An additional achievement to that of Rogers, however, is that Beck has managed to do this within the state psychiatric system, where it may be argued that the need is greatest. Rogers, by contrast, conducted an unsuccessful experiment in the Mendota hospital and retreated from the psychiatric arena thereafter. Another therapy model that had succeeded in the psychiatric system was behaviour therapy. At the time of Beck's rise to fame, behaviour therapy was in tem-porary decline, whereas, as was argued earlier in alliance with cognitive therapy, it has since revived and flourished.

Of course, no theory is perfect and two areas of Beck's work stand out to me as unsatisfactory. The first is that of the evolutionary concept, which as I argued earlier, seems to me intriguing but insufficiently developed – perhaps exemplified by the small number of lines devoted to explaining the rather big concepts of 'mode' and 'charge' (Beck, 1996). The second, which has attracted more academic criticism than the first, is the central one of cognitive change mechanisms. We noted the criticisms of the schema concept, and, more recently, a number of critics have started to suggest that the cognitive focus may not be very important (Bennett-Levy, 2003; Hayes et al., 2004; Longmore & Worrell, 2007). These criticisms seem potentially fatal to cognitive therapy. Some of these criticisms have emerged from 'dismantling' studies in which the separate elements of therapy are tested to find which are the 'active' elements. It has been difficult to show an independent additive effect for purely cognitive interventions. This is the usual complicated research story, but my view on this is that a 'purely cognitive approach' would be unlikely to be pursued by many cognitive therapists. Beck has been very committed to integrating a behavioural dimension into cognitive therapy. It is interesting that the real moment of conversion away from psychoanalysis seems to have come from the *behavioural* testing of the 'retroflected hostility' hypothesis – the depressed subjects in the research were reinforced by success just as much as the non-depressed (Loeb et al., 1964). Salient cognitions frequently have a behavioural disposition in them so that engagement with them is likely to influence behaviour, though this may take time to show itself. Perhaps cognitive therapists have overstated the rationale of behavioural experiments. As I noted earlier, it seems likely to me that changes in clients' behaviour may be *both* significant as changed behaviours in themselves and as disconfirmations of negative beliefs.

As Beck moved from psychoanalysis, he seems to have experienced significant cognitive dissonance himself (Salkovskis, 1996a). Fortunately, he has also shown willingness to work on his own thoughts and feelings (Padesky, 2004). This stance may have been behind his strong commitment to collaboration in therapeutic practice. Collaboration is evident in shared agenda setting and taking feedback from clients on a regular basis. Thus, although cognitive therapy is quite directive, proper respect for collaboration prevents any tendency towards authoritarian practice. The characteristic Socratic style of questioning is designed not to 'extract' assessment information but to stimulate the client to recognise his own way of thinking and also to stimulate new information to balance negative conclusions. The purpose is not to achieve change by debating cognitions but to bring the client to the point where he sees the relativity of some of his thoughts and to desire to test out their validity and/or utility.

People viewing Beck's various therapy tapes often comment on the quality of his listening skills and his gentle reflective approach (Padesky, 2004; Salkovskis, 1996a), so that sometimes viewers who hold the stereotype of overly directive CBT think that Beck cannot be doing it! When checked against the checklist of cognitive therapy skills (Young & Beck, 1980), it can be seen that he has done the therapy – but with a light touch.

The fact that therapist skills and interventions can also be checked against skill inventories and protocols is another great gift that Beck has given to the therapy world, along with other factors that have emerged from his elegant research, such as valid measures, best exemplified by the BDI, and especially his practice of refraining from publishing protocols and procedures until they have been properly researched and tested.

Cognitive therapy theory has sometimes been accused of lacking insight into social and political power. This implies that it has a 'ten per cent conservatism' bias. At its crudest, we are accused of eliminating surface symptoms and problems and refitting clients back into an oppressive society. Critics imply that therapy should have a social critical perspective. This strikes me as both 'grandstanding' and lacking an appreciation of both social and individual power. Therapists who do not recognise or attempt to harness their influence may be dangerous, but perhaps not much more dangerous than those who have delusions about their ability to get clients to do what they are not open to doing. Cognitive therapists follow in an honourable tradition, started by the behaviourists, of challenging psychiatric 'labelling' not by suggesting that clients are victims but rather by ensuring that there are reliable treatments based on individual needs rather than reductionist labels. Although Beck has followed the symptoms groupings suggested by the *DSM*, he has addressed the most serious gap in the *DSM* by defining underlying cognitive profiles to support proper formulation of therapy treatment, instead of relying on tired old symptom descriptions. The behaviourists began such individual formulation (Bruch & Bond, 1998) but only in very limited areas such as phobias (Padesky, 2004). Beck has 'supplied the content' to behavioural treatment and has thus greatly widened treatment options for millions of psychiatric patients and therapy clients worldwide. This, in my view, has been a much more profound contribution than standing on the sidelines merely making 'anti-psychiatry' noises.

On a personal level, Beck has been an inspiring figure to a global cognitive therapy community. This has involved having vision – in this case a global vision of a therapy movement that has exercised influence by the strength of its case. He has been an alliance builder and at times an astute player. At a time when many of his peers rejected his ideas, he cultivated bright, younger researchers and ensured a rising generation attuned to his ideas. This was a two-way street: they benefited from his patronage and he benefited from building an army of foot soldiers – many with officer potential. His personal charm and social skills at listening and responding to friends and foes alike greatly aided this process of alliance building – and who would not consider him as 'first name on team sheet' when putting a team together? The global reach of his influence is symbolised by the fact that when considering setting up an American association, he rather chose to start an international one – the World Congress of Cognitive Therapy (Padesky, 2004). He strikes most people as a decent and modest man – but may not be above occasionally using the 'mock modesty' tactic of Socrates to advantage! His work has no element of 'flash in the pan'. It has been meticulously built for half a century – a slow 'pooling' of concepts and practices (Padesky, 2004) that has proved all the more convincing for the 'slow burn' of its development. He has put few fences round his work, and the easy access to him and his ideas has allowed many to follow in his footsteps and build on his work. There has been a pleasant degree of camaraderie about this process; it is sometimes difficult to find who came up with which idea when.

Finally, Beck is approaching his eighty-seventh birthday as I write. In recent years, he might have been expected to rest on the laurels of creating an impressive worldwide therapy movement – in fact, his output has hardly seemed to flag. Goodness only knows what else he might achieve in his career!

As I was writing this book about him, I picked up my first free bus pass.[1] I started to notice certain thoughts such as 'Perhaps this will be my last contribution to the field' slide through my mind. Negative thoughts? Not me – I am a genuine 'old-timer'! As I surveyed Beck's publication record, however, I began to realise that by 60 he had hardly got going! So perhaps I will continue to trouble the public with my thoughts on therapy yet awhile! If I can at least aspire to even a small degree of the sense, grace and wit of Aaron T. Beck, then I can consider it time well spent!

Note

1 Attained in England at the age of 60.

References

Alford, B. A. & Beck, A. T. (1997) *The integrative power of cognitive therapy*. New York: Guilford Press.

American Psychiatric Association (APA) (2000) *Diagnostic and statistical manual of mental disorders* (4th edn, text revision). Washington, DC: APA.

Bandura, A. (1969) *Principles of behaviour modification*. New York/London: Holt, Rinehart & Winston.

Beck, A. T. (1963) Thinking and depression. Part I: Idiosyncratic content and cognitive distortions. *Archives of General Psychiatry*, 9: 324–333.

Beck, A. T. (1964) Thinking and depression. Part II: Theory and therapy. *Archives of General Psychiatry*, 10: 561–571.

Beck, A. T. (1967) *Depression: Clinical, experimental and theoretical aspects*. New York: Harper & Row.

Beck, A. T. (1970a) The role of fantasies in psychotherapy and psychopathology. *Journal of Nervous and Mental Disease*, 150: 3–17.

Beck, A. T. (1970b) Cognitive therapy: Nature and relation to behavior therapy. *Behavior Therapy*, 1(2): 184–200.

Beck, A. T. (1976) *Cognitive therapy and the emotional disorders*. Harmondsworth, UK: Penguin.

Beck, A. T. (1979) Schools of 'thought' (comment on Wolpe's 'Cognition and causation in human behavior and its therapy'). *American Psychologist*, 34: 93–98.

Beck, A. T. (1987) Cognitive models of depression. *Journal of Cognitive Psychotherapy: An International Quarterly*, 1: 5–38.

Beck, A. T. (1988) *Love is never enough*. Harmondsworth, UK: Penguin.

Beck, A. T. (1991) Cognitive therapy: A 30-year retrospective. *American Psychologist*, 46(4): 368–375.

Beck, A. T. (1996) Beyond belief: A theory of modes, personality and psychotherapy. In P. M. Salkovskis (Ed.), *Frontiers of cognitive therapy* (pp. 1–25). New York: Guilford Press.

Beck, A. T. (1999) Cognitive aspects of personality disorders and their relation to syndromal disorders: A psycho-evolutionary approach. In C. R. Cloninger (Ed.), *Personality and psychopathology* (pp. 411–429). Washington, DC: American Psychiatric Press.

Beck, A. T. (2002) Cognitive models of depression. In R. L. Leahy & E. T. Dowd (Eds.), *Clinical advances in cognitive psychotherapy: Theories and applications* (pp. 29–61). New York: Springer.

Beck, A. T. (2004) A cognitive model of schizophrenia. *Journal of Cognitive Psychotherapy*, 18: 281–288.

Beck, A. T. (2005a) The current state of cognitive therapy: A 40-year retrospective. *Archives of General Psychiatry*, 62(9): 953–959.

Beck, A. T. (2005b) Buddhism and cognitive therapy. www.beck institute.org, Spring 2005, accessed 28 March 2008.

Beck, A. T. & Valin, S. (1953) Psychotic depressive reactions in soldiers who accidentally killed their buddies. *American Journal of Psychiatry*, 110: 347–353.

Beck, A. T. & Hurvich, M. S. (1959) Psychological correlates of depression. I: Frequency of 'masochistic' dream content in a private practice sample. *Psychometric Medicine*, 21: 50–55.

Beck, A. T., Ward, C. H., Mendelson, M., Mock, J. & Erbaugh, J. (1961) An inventory for measuring depression. *Archives of General Psychiatry*, 4: 562–571.

Beck, A. T., Laude, R., Bohnert, M. (1974a) Ideational components of anxiety neurosis. *Archives of General Psychiatry*, 31: 319–325.

Beck, A. T., Schuyler, D. & Herman, J. (1974b) Development of suicidal intent scales. In A. T. Beck, H. L. P. Resnik & D. J. Lettieri (Eds.), *The prediction of suicide* (pp. 45–56). Bowie, MD: Charles Press.

Beck, A. T., Kovacs, M. & Weissman, A. (1975) Hopelessness and suicidal behaviour: An overview. *Journal of the American Medical Association*, 234: 1146–1149.

Beck, A. T., Kovacs, M. & Weissman, A. (1979a) Assessment of suicidal intention: The Scale for Suicidal Ideation. *Journal of Consulting and Clinical Psychology*, 47(2): 343–352.

Beck, A. T., Shaw, B. E., Rush, A. J. & Emery, G. (1979b) *Cognitive therapy of depression*. New York: Guilford Press.

Beck, A. T. & Emery, G. with Greenberg, R. (1985) *Anxiety disorders and phobias: A cognitive perspective.* New York: Basic Books.

Beck, A. T., Epstein, N., Brown, G. & Steer, R. A. (1988) An inventory for measuring clinical anxiety: Psychometric properties. *Journal of Consulting and Clinical Psychology*, 47: 343–352.

Beck, A. T., Freeman, A. & Associates (1990) *Cognitive therapy of personality disorders.* New York: Guilford Press.

Beck, A. T., Wright, F. D., Newman, C. F. & Liese, B. S. (1993) *Cognitive therapy of substance abuse.* New York: Guilford Press.

Beck, A. T., Baruch, E., Balter, J. M., Steer, R. A. & Warman, D. M. (2004) A new instrument for measuring insight: The Beck Cognitive Insight Scale. *Schizophrenia Research*, 68: 319–329.

Beck, A. T., Freeman, A. & Associates (Eds.) (2004) *Cognitive therapy of personality disorders* (rev. edn). New York: Guilford Press.

Beck, J. (1995) *Cognitive therapy: Basics and beyond.* New York: Guilford Press.

Bennett-Levy, J. (2003) Mechanisms of change in cognitive therapy: The case of automatic thought records and behavioural experiments. *Behavioural and Cognitive Psychotherapy*, 31: 261–277.

Bennett-Levy, J. (2006) Therapist skills: A cognitive model of their acquisition and refinement. *Behavioural and Cognitive Psychotherapy*, 34(1): 57–78.

Bennett-Levy, J., Butler, G., Fennell, M., Hackmann, A., Mueller, M. & Westbrook, D. (2004) *Oxford guide to behavioural experiments.* Oxford, UK: Oxford University Press.

Bennett-Levy, J. & Thwaites, R. (2006) Self and self-reflection in the therapeutic relationship: A conceptual map and practical strategies for the training, supervision and self-supervision of interpersonal skills. In P. Gilbert. & R. Leahy (Eds.), *The therapeutic relationship in the cognitive behavioural psychotherapies* (pp. 255–281). London: Routledge.

Bennett-Levy, J. & Beedie, A. (2007) The ups and downs of cognitive therapy training: What happens to trainees' perception of their competence during a cognitive therapy training course? *Behavioural and Cognitive Psychotherapy*, 35: 61–75.

Beutler, L. E., Machado, P. & Neufeld, S. (1994) Therapist variables. In A. E. Bergin & S. L. Garfield (Eds.), *Handbook of psychotherapy and behaviour change* (pp. 230–265). New York: John Wiley & Sons.

Brewin, C. R. (1996) Theoretical foundations of cognitive behaviour therapy for anxiety and depression. *Annual Review of Psychology*, 47: 33–57.

Brown, B. M. (1967) Cognitive aspects of Wolpe's behavior therapy. *American Journal of Psychiatry*, 124(6): 854–859.

Brown, G. K., Beck, A. T., Steer, R. A. & Grisham, J. R. (2000) Risk factors for suicide in psychiatric outpatients: A 20-year prospective study. *Journal of Consulting and Clinical Psychology*, 68(3): 371–377.

Bruch, M. & Bond, F. W. (1998) *Beyond diagnosis: Case formulation approaches in CBT*. Chichester, UK: John Wiley & Sons.

Burns, D. D. (1999) *The feeling good handbook* (rev. edn). New York: Penguin.

Butler, G. & Hope, D. (2006) *Manage your mind* (2nd edn). Oxford, UK: Oxford University Press.

Cahill, J. (1996) Patient participation: A concept analysis. *Journal of Advanced Nursing*, 24(3): 561–571.

Clark, D. A. & Steer, R. A. (1996) Empirical status of the cognitive model of anxiety and depression. In P. M. Salkovskis (Ed.), *Frontiers of cognitive therapy* (pp. 75–96). New York: Guilford Press.

Clark, D. A. & Beck, A. T. (2002) *Clark-Beck Obsessive Compulsive Inventory Manual*. San Antonio, TX: The Psychological Corporation.

Clark, D. M. (1996) Panic disorder: From theory to therapy. In P. M. Salkovskis (Ed.), *Frontiers of cognitive therapy* (pp. 318–344). New York: Guilford Press.

Clarkson, P. & Mackewn, J. (1993) *Fritz Perls*. London: Sage.

Cummings, N. & Sayama, M. (1995) *Focused psychotherapy: A casebook of brief, intermittent psychotherapy through the life cycle*. New York: Brunner/Mazel.

Department of Health (2008) *Improving access to psychological therapies implementation plan: National guidelines for regional delivery*. London: DoH.

Dobson, K. S. & Shaw, B. F. (1993) The training of cognitive therapists: What have we learnt from treatment manuals? *Journal of Clinical and Consulting Psychology*, 56(5): 673–680.

Dryden, W. (1991) *Against dogma: A dialogue with Albert Ellis*. Milton Keynes, UK: Open University Press.

Dryden, W. (1995) *Brief rational emotive behaviour therapy*. Chichester, UK: John Wiley & Sons.

Dryden, W. (1998) *Are you sitting uncomfortably? Windy Dryden: Live and uncut*. Ross-on-Wye, UK: PCCS Books.

Dryden, W. (2004) *Rational emotive behaviour therapy in Action*. London: Sage.

Dryden, W. & Hill, L. K. (1992) *Innovations in rational-emotive therapy*. Newbury Park, CA: Sage.

D'Zurilla, T. J. & Nezu, A. M. (1999) *Problem-solving therapy: A social competence approach to clinical intervention* (2nd edn). New York: Springer.

Edelman, S. (2006) *Change your thinking: Overcome stress, combat anxiety and improve your life with CBT*. London: Vermillion.

Edwards, D. J. A. (1990) Cognitive therapy and the restructuring of early memories through guided imagery. *Journal of Cognitive Psychotherapy: An International Quarterly*, 4(1): 33–50.

Eells, T. C. (Ed.) (1997) *Handbook of psychotherapy case formulation*. New York: Guilford Press.

Ehlers, A. & Clark, D. M. (2000) A cognitive model of posttraumatic stress disorder. *Behaviour Research and Therapy*, 38: 319–345.

Ellis, A. (1962) *Reason and emotion in psychotherapy*. Syracuse, NY: Citadel.

Ellis, A. (1977) *Anger – how to live with it and without it*. Secaucus, NJ: Citadel.

Ellis, A. (1979) On Joseph Wolpe's espousal of cognitive-behavior therapy (letter). *American Psychologist*, 34: 98–99.

Ellis, A. & Dryden, W. (1987) *The practice of rational-emotive therapy*. New York: Springer.

Emery, G. (1999) *Overcoming depression: Therapist's manual*. Oakland, CA: New Harbinger.

Epstein, S. (1998) *Constructive thinking: The key to emotional intelligence*. Westport, CT: Praeger.

Espie, C. A. (2006) *Overcoming insomnia and sleep problems*. London: Robinson.

Eysenck, M. (1997) *Anxiety and emotion: A unified theory*. Hove, UK: Psychology Press.

Feltham, C. (Ed.) (1999) *Understanding the counselling relationship*. London: Sage.

Fennell, M. J. V. (1989) Depression. In K. Hawton, P. M. Salkovskis, J. Kirk & D. M. Clark (Eds.), *Cognitive behaviour therapy for psychiatric problems* (pp. 169–234). Oxford, UK: Oxford Medical Publications.

Fennell, M. J. V. (2004) Depression, low self esteem and mindfulness. *Behaviour Therapy and Research*, 42: 1053–1067.

Festinger, L. (1957) *A theory of cognitive dissonance*. Evanston, IL: Row Peterson.

Foa, B. & Kozak, M. (1986) Emotional processing of fear: Exposure to corrective information. *Psychological Bulletin*, 99: 20–35.

Frude, N. (2005) Prescription for a good read. *Counselling and Psychotherapy Journal*, 16(1): 28–31.

Furneaux, R. (1973) *The Roman siege of Jerusalem*. London: Hart-Davis MacGibbon.

Gendlin, E. (1981) *Focusing*. New York: Everest House.

Gerth, H. H. & Wright Mills, C. (1991) *From Max Weber: Essays in sociology* (2nd edn). London: Routledge.

Gilbert, P. (1989) *Human nature and suffering.* Hove, UK: Lawrence Erlbaum Associates, Ltd.

Gilbert, P. (1998) The evolved basis and adaptive functions of cognitive distortions. *British Journal of Medical Psychology*, 71: 447–463.

Gilbert, P. (2006) A biosocial and evolutionary approach to formulation with a special focus on shame. In N. Tarrier (Ed.), *Case formulation in CBT: The treatment of challenging and complex cases* (pp. 81–112). London: Routledge.

Gilbert, P. (2007) Evolved minds and compassion. In P. Gilbert & R. L. Leahy (Eds.), *The therapeutic relationship in the cognitive behavioural psychotherapies* (pp. 106–142). London: Routledge.

Gilbert, P. & Andrews, B. (Eds.) (1998) *Shame: Interpersonal behavior, psychopathology and culture.* New York: Oxford University Press.

Goode, E. (2000) Scientist at work: Aaron T. Beck: Pragmatist embodies his no-nonsense therapy. *New York Times*, 11 January 2000.

Greenberg, L. S. (2002) *Emotion-focused therapy: Coaching clients to work through their feelings.* Washington, DC: APA.

Greenberg, L. S. (2007) Emotion in the therapeutic relationship in emotion-focused therapy. In R. L. Leahy & P. Gilbert (Eds.), *The therapeutic relationship in the cognitive behavioural psychotherapies* (pp. 43–62). London: Routledge.

Greenberger, D. & Padesky, C. (1995) *Mind over mood.* New York: Guilford Press.

Hackmann, A. & Holmes, E. A. (2004) Reflections on imagery: A clinical perspective and review of the special edition of *Memory* on using imagery in psychotherapy. *Memory*, 12(4): 389–402.

Harvey, A. G. (2002) A cognitive model of insomnia. *Behaviour Research and Therapy*, 40: 869–893.

Hawton, K., Salkovskis, P. M., Kirk, J. & Clark, D. (1989) *Cognitive behaviour therapy for psychiatric problems.* Oxford, UK: Blackwell.

Hayes, S. C., Strohsal, K. D. & Wilson, K. D. (2004) *Acceptance and commitment therapy: An experiential guide.* New York: Guilford Press.

Hersen, M. (Ed.) (2002) *Clinical behaviour therapy: Adults and children.* New York: John Wiley & Sons.

Hollon, S. D., DeRubeis, R. J. & Evans, M. D. (1996) Cognitive therapy in the treatment and prevention of depression. In P. M. Salkovskis (Ed.), *Frontiers of cognitive therapy* (pp. 293–317). New York: Guilford Press.

Hollon, S. D. & Kendall, P. C. (1980) Cognitive self-statements in depression: Development of automatic thoughts questionnaire. *Cognitive Therapy and Research*, 4(4): 383–395.

Holmes, J. (2000) NHS psychotherapy: Past, present and future. *British Journal of Psychotherapy*, 16(2): 154–175.

Hudson, B. L. & Macdonald, G. M. (1986) *Behavioural social work*. Basingstoke, UK: Macmillan.

Ivey, A. E., Ivey, M. B. & Simek-Morgan, L. (1997) *Counselling and psychotherapy: Skills, theory and practice*. New York: Prentice-Hall International.

Jacobs, M. (2006) *The presenting past: The core of psychodynamic counselling and psychotherapy* (3rd edn). Milton Keynes, UK: Open University Press.

Jacobson, N. S. & Hollon, S. D. (1999a) Cognitive therapy versus pharmacology: Now the jury has returned its verdict, it is time for the rest of the evidence. *Journal of Consulting and Clinical Psychology*, 64: 74–80.

Jacobson, N. S. & Hollon, S. D. (1999b) Prospects for future comparisons between drugs and psychotherapy: Lessons from the CBT vs. pharmacology exchange. *Journal of Consulting and Clinical Psychology*, 64: 104–108.

Johnstone, L. & Dallos, R. (2006) *Formulation in psychology and psychotherapy*. London: Routledge.

Kabat-Zinn, J. (2001) *Full catastrophe living*. New York: Piatkus.

Kazantzis, N. (2000) Power to detect homework effects in psychotherapy outcome research. *Journal of Consulting and Clinical Psychology*, 68(1): 166–170.

Kazantzis, N., Deane, F. P. & Ronan, K. R. (2000) Homework assignments in cognitive and behavioural therapy: A meta-analysis. *Clinical Psychology: Science and Practice*, 7: 182–192.

Kazantzis, N., Deane, F. P., Ronan, K. R. & L'Abate, L. (Eds.) (2005a) *Using homework assignments in cognitive behaviour therapy*. New York: Routledge.

Kazantzis, N., Lampropoulos, G. K. & Deane, F. P. (2005b) A national survey of practising psychologists use of and attitudes towards homework in psychotherapy. *Journal of Consulting and Clinical Psychology*, 73(4): 742–748.

Kazantzis, N. & Ronan, K. R. (2006) Can between session (homework) activities be considered a common factor for psychotherapy? *Journal of Psychotherapy Integration*, 16(2): 189–192.

Kiejsers, G. P., Schaap, C. P. & Hoogduin, C. A. (2000) The impact of interpersonal patient and therapist behaviour on outcome in cognitive behaviour therapy: A review of empirical studies. *Behaviour Modification*, 24(2): 264–297.

Kiesler, R. J. (1966) Some myths of psychotherapy research and the search for paradigm. In A. P. Goldstein & N. Stein (Eds.), *Prescriptive psychotherapy* (pp. 102–126). New York: Pergamon.

Kirschenbaum, H. & Henderson, V. L. (Eds.) (1990) *Carl Rogers dialogues*. London: Constable.

Kovacs, M. & Beck, A. T. (1978) Maladaptive cognitive structures in depression. *American Journal of Psychiatry*, 135: 525–533.

Kuyken, W. (2006) Evidence-based formulation: Is the emperor clothed? In N. Tarrier (Ed.), *Case formulation in cognitive behaviour therapy* (pp. 12–35). London: Routledge.

Lang, P. J. (1977) Imagery in therapy: An information processing and analysis of fear. *Behavior Therapy*, 8(5): 862–836.

Layden, M. A. (1998) UWN workshop.

Layden, M. A., Newman, C. F., Freeman, A. & Morse, S. B. (1993) *Cognitive therapy of borderline personality disorder*. Boston, MA: Allyn & Bacon.

Leahy, R. L. (2001) *Overcoming resistance in cognitive therapy*. New York: Guilford Press.

Leahy, R. L. (2003) *Cognitive therapy techniques*. New York: Guilford Press.

Leahy, R. L. (2005) *The worry cure: Stop worrying and start living.* London: Piatkus.

Lewinsohn, P. M. & Graf, M. (1973) Pleasant activities and depression. *Journal of Consulting and Clinical Psychology*, 4(1): 261–268.

Linehan, M. M. (1993) *Cognitive behavioural treatment for borderline personality disorder*. New York: Guilford Press.

Linklater, R. J. & Harland, R. (2006) After Freud. *Prospect Magazine*, 123: 36–41.

Liotti, G. (1991) Patterns of attachment and the assessment of interpersonal schemata: Understanding and changing difficult patient–therapist relationships in cognitive psychotherapy. *Journal of Cognitive Psychotherapy*, 5: 105–114.

Liotti, G. (2007) Internal working models of attachment. In P. Gilbert & R. L. Leahy (Eds.), *The therapeutic relationship in the cognitive behavioural psychotherapies* (pp. 143–161). London: Routledge.

Loeb, A., Beck, A. T., Feshbach, S. & Wolf, A. (1964) Some aspects of regard upon the social perceptions and motivation of psychiatric patients with depression. *Journal of Abnormal Psychology*, 68: 609–616.

Longmore, R. J. & Worrell, M. (2007) Do we need to challenge thoughts on cognitive behaviour therapy? *Clinical Psychology Review*, 27: 173–187.

Mackay, H. C., West, W., Moorey, J., Guthrie, E. & Margison, F.

(2001) Counsellors' experiences of changing their practice: Learning the psychodynamic-interpersonal model of therapy. *Counselling and Psychotherapy Research*, 1(1): 29–35.

March, P. (1997) In two minds about cognitive therapy? *British Journal of Psychotherapy*, 13(4): 461–472.

Milne, D. L., Baker, C., Blackburn, I.-M., James, I. & Reichelt, K. F. (1999) The effectiveness of cognitive therapy training. *Journal of Behaviour Therapy and Experimental Psychiatry*, 30(2): 81–92.

Milne, D. L., Claydon, T., Blackburn, I.-M., James, I. & Sheikh, A. (2001) Rationale for a new measure of competence in therapy. *Behavioural and Cognitive Psychotherapies*, 29: 21–33.

Milton, J. (2001) Psychoanalysis and cognitive behaviour therapy – rival paradigms or common ground? *International Journal of Psychoanalysis*, 82: 431–447.

Mooney, K. & Padesky, C. A. (1998) Between two minds: The transformational power of underlying assumptions. Workshop presentation at the European Association of Cognitive Behaviour Therapy, Cork, September 1998.

Orlinsky, D. E., Grawe, K. & Parks, B. K. (1994) Process and outcome in psychotherapy – noch einmal. In A. E. Bergin & S. L. Garfield (Eds.), *Handbook of psychotherapy and behaviour change* (4th edn) (pp. 270–378). New York: John Wiley & Sons.

Padesky, C. A. (1994) *Cognitive therapy of anxiety* (audio tape). Newport Beach, CA: Center for Cognitive Therapy, www.padesky.com

Padesky, C. A. (1996) Developing cognitive therapy competency: Training and supervision models. In P. M. Salkovskis (Ed.), *Frontiers of cognitive therapy* (pp. 262–292). New York: Guilford Press.

Padesky, C. A. (2004) Aaron T. Beck: Mind, man and mentor. In R. L. Leahy (Ed.), *Contemporary cognitive therapy: Theory, research and practice* (pp. 3–23). New York: Guilford Press.

Padesky, C. A. & Beck, A. T. (1990) *Love is never enough* (audio tape). Newport Beach, CA: Center for Cognitive Therapy, www.padesky.com

Padesky, C. A. & Greenberger, D. (1995) *A clinician's guide to mind over mood.* New York: Guilford Press.

Padesky, C. A. & Beck, A. T. (2003) Science and philosophy: Comparison of cognitive therapy and rational emotive behavior therapy. *Journal of Clinical Psychology*, 17(3): 211–224.

Papageorgiou, C. & Wells, A. (2003) *Depressive ruminations.* Chichester, UK: John Wiley & Sons.

Persons, J. B. (1989) *Cognitive therapy: A case formulation approach.* New York: W. W. Norton.

Persons, J. B. (2005) Empiricism, mechanism, and the practice of cognitive-behavior therapy. *Behavior Therapy*, 36: 107–118.

Persons, J. B., Gross, J. J., Etkin, M. S. & Madan, S. K. (1996) Psychodynamic therapists' reservations about cognitive-behaviour therapy: Implications for training and practice. *Journal of Psychotherapy Practice and Research*, 5: 202–212.

Psychological and Educational Films (1986) *Three approaches to psychotherapy: Richard.* Corona Del Mar, CA: Psychological and Educational Films.

Rachman, S. (1997a) The evolution of CBT. In D. M. Clark & C. Fairburn (Eds.), *The science and practice of CBT* (pp. 3–26). Oxford, UK: Oxford University Press.

Rachman, S. (1997b) *Anxiety.* Hove, UK: Psychology Press.

Rachman, S. (2003) *The treatment of obsessions.* Oxford, UK: Oxford University Press.

Rachman, S. & da Silva, P. (1978) Abnormal and normal obsessions. *Behaviour Therapy and Research*, 16: 233–248.

Reichelt, K. F., James, I. A. & Blackburn, I.-M. (2003) The impact of training for rating competency in cognitive therapy. *Journal of Behavioural, Therapeutic and Experimental Psychiatry*, 34(2): 87–99.

Rogers, C. R. (1957) The necessary and sufficient conditions for therapeutic personality change. *Journal of Consulting Psychology*, 21(2): 95–113.

Rogers, C. R. (1980) *A way of being.* Boston, MA: Houghton-Mifflin.

Roth, A. & Fonagy, P. (2005) *What works for whom: A critical review of psychotherapy research* (2nd edn). New York: Guilford Press.

Roth, A. & Pilling, S. (2007) *The competencies required to deliver effective cognitive and behavioural therapy for people with depression and with anxiety.* London: Department of Health.

Rush, A. J. & Watkins, J. T. (1977) Specialised cognitive therapy strategies for psychologically naive depressed outpatients. Paper given at the Conference of the American Psychological Association, San Francisco, CA, August 1977.

Safran, J. D. & Muran, J. C. (2000) *Negotiating the therapeutic alliance: A relational treatment guide.* New York: Guilford.

Safran, J. D. & Segal, Z. V. (1990) *Interpersonal processes and cognitive therapy.* New York: Guilford Press.

Salkovskis, P. M. (1991) The importance of behaviour in the maintenance of anxiety and panic: A cognitive account. *Behavioural Psychotherapy*, 19: 6–19.

Salkovskis, P. M. (1996a) Anxiety, beliefs and safety-seeking behaviour. In P. M. Salkovskis (Ed.), *Frontiers of cognitive therapy* (pp. 48–74). New York: Guilford Press.

Salkovskis, P. M. (1996b) Cognitive therapy and Aaron T. Beck. In P. M. Salkovskis (Ed.), *Frontiers of cognitive therapy* (pp. 532–539). New York: Guilford Press.

Salkovskis, P. M., Forrester, E., Richards, H. C. & Morrison, N. (1998) The devil is in the detail: Conceptualising and treating obsessional problems. In N. Tarrier (Ed.), *Treating complex cases: The cognitive behavioural approach* (pp. 46–80). Chichester, UK: John Wiley & Sons.

Sanders, D. & Wills, F. (2003) *Counselling for anxiety problems.* London: Sage.

Sanders, D. & Wills, F. (2005) *Cognitive therapy: An introduction.* London: Sage.

Sanders, P. (2004) Some powerful ideas in counselling. Keynote address, Counselling conference, University of Wales, Newport, June 2004.

Segal, Z. V., Williams, J. M. G. & Teasdale, J. D. (2002) *Mindfulness based cognitive therapy: A new approach to preventing relapse.* New York: Guilford Press.

Shaw, B. F., Elkin, I., Yamaguchi, J., Lomsted, M., Vallis, T. M., Dobson, K. S. et al. (1999) Therapist competency ratings in relation to clinical outcome in cognitive therapy of depression. *Journal of Clinical and Consulting Psychology*, 67: 837–846.

Sheldon, B. (1995) *Cognitive behaviour therapy: Research, practice and philosophy.* London: Routledge.

Simmons, M. & Wills, F. (2006) *CBT skills in practice* (video/DVD). Newport, UK: University of Wales, Newport.

Spong, S. & Hollanders, H. (2003) Cognitive therapy and social power. *Counselling and Psychotherapy Research*, 3(3): 216–227.

Stevenson, A. (Ed.) (2007) *Shorter Oxford English Dictionary.* Oxford, UK: Oxford University Press.

Stricker, G. (2006) Using homework in psychodynamic psychotherapy. *Journal of Psychotherapy Integration*, 16(2): 219–237.

Sudak, D. M., Beck, J. S. & Wright, J. (2003) Cognitive behavior therapy: A blueprint for attaining and assessing psychiatric resident competency. *Academic Psychiatry*, 27: 143–159.

Teasdale, J. D. (1996) Clinically relevant theory: Integrating clinical insight into cognitive science. In P. M. Salkovskis (Ed.), *Frontiers of cognitive therapy* (pp. 26–47). New York: Guilford Press.

Trepka, C., Rees, A., Shapiro, D. A., Hardy, G. E. & Barkham, M. (2004) Therapist competency and outcome of cognitive therapy of depression. *Cognitive Therapy and Research*, 28(2): 154–159.

Van Deurzen-Smith, E. (2002) *Existential counselling and psychotherapy* (2nd edn). London: Sage.

Vitousek, K. M. (1996) The current status of cognitive-behavioural models of anorexia nervosa and bulimia nervosa. In P. M. Salkovskis (Ed.), *Frontiers of cognitive therapy* (pp. 383–418). New York: Guilford Press.

Weishaar, M. (1993) *Aaron T. Beck*. London: Sage.

Weishaar, M. & Beck, A. T. (1992) Clinical and cognitive predictors of suicide. In R. W. Maris, A. L. Berman, J. T. Mattisberger & R. I. Yufit (Eds.), *Assessment and prediction of suicide* (pp. 487–483). New York: Guilford Press.

Wells, A. (1997) *Cognitive therapy of anxiety disorders*. Chichester, UK: John Wiley & Sons.

Wells, A. (2000) *Emotional disorders and metacognition*. Chichester, UK: John Wiley & Sons.

Wells, A. (2006) Cognitive therapy case formulation in anxiety disorders. In N. Tarrier (Ed.), *Case formulation in cognitive behaviour therapy* (pp. 52–80). Hove, UK: Routledge.

Wells, A. & Mathews, G. (1994) *Attention and emotion: A clinical perspective*. Hove, UK: Lawrence Erlbaum Associates Ltd.

Williams, C. (2002) Using structured cognitive behavioural therapy self-help materials in a clinical service. *Psychiatry*, 1(3): 28–31.

Williams, J. M. G. (1996) Memory processes in psychotherapy. In P. Salkovskis (Ed.), *Frontiers of cognitive therapy* (pp. 97–113). New York: Guilford Press.

Williams, R. M., Moorey, S. & Cobb, J. (1991) Training in cognitive therapy: A pilot evaluation using the cognitive therapy scale. *Journal of Behavioural Psychotherapy*, 19: 373–376.

Williams, S. J., Calnan, M. & Gabe, J. (2000) *Health, medicine and society: Key theories, future agendas*. London: Routledge.

Wills, F. (2006) CBT: Can counsellors fill the gap? *Healthcare Counselling and Psychotherapy Journal*, 6(2): 6–9.

Wills, F. (2008) *Skills in cognitive behavioural counselling and psychotherapy*. London: Sage.

Wolpe, J. (1958) *Psychotherapy by reciprocal inhibition*. Stanford, CA: Stanford University Press.

Wolpe, J. (1978) Cognition and causation in human behaviour and its therapy. *American Psychologist*, 33: 437–446.

Young, J. E. & Beck, A. T. (1980) *The cognitive therapy scale*. Philadelphia, PA: Center for Cognitive Therapy.

Young, J. E. & Beck, A. T. (1988) *The cognitive therapy scale* (rev. edn). Philadelphia, PA: Center for Cognitive Therapy.

Young, J. E., Klosko, J. S. & Weishaar, M. (2003), *Schema therapy: A practitioner's guide*. New York: Guilford Press.

Index